Penetrating Polarization and Winning the Ohio Governorship in 2006

Penetrating Polarization and Winning the Ohio Governorship in 2006

◆

A Guide for Concerned Citizens

A "Grassroots Guide" to Enhance the Electability of Ted Strickland for Governor

Vernon Lucas Albright, Ed.D.
and
Mary Helen Albright, M.A.

iUniverse, Inc.
New York Lincoln Shanghai

Penetrating Polarization and Winning the Ohio Governorship in 2006
A Guide for Concerned Citizens

iUniverse books may be ordered through booksellers or by contacting:

iUniverse
2021 Pine Lake Road, Suite 100
Lincoln, NE 68512
www.iuniverse.com
1-800-Authors (1-800-288-4677)

ISBN-13: 978-0-595-41070-5 (pbk)
ISBN-13: 978-0-595-85430-1 (ebk)
ISBN-10: 0-595-41070-7 (pbk)
ISBN-10: 0-595-85430-3 (ebk)

Printed in the United States of America

To Mary Helen Albright

The most important person in my life is my wife, Mary Helen Albright for whom this book is dedicated. As she has said, and I agree:
"I am her ticket to Heaven." I might add that "sainthood" would also be appropriate for her as well.

"If you have a big idea, do the big idea."

—**Professor Gabriel Almond**
1911–2002
Professor of Political Science
Stanford University

Contents

Preface xiii

Part I   *An Introduction to Winning Elections*

CHAPTER 1   Guidelines for Democrats to Win the Governorship
in 2006 3

CHAPTER 2   Age, Demographics, and Policy Issues
(Ages 18 to 100+) 9

CHAPTER 3   Watch your Backsides and Beware of the...
"Moral Majority". 13

CHAPTER 4   A Series of Value Systems for Case Studies in Ohio
Representing Changing Family Value Systems
Over the Next Generation ("Style"
Challenges—Family and Community Moral Issues
Affecting the Democrats and Republican Value
Systems) 20

CHAPTER 5   "Traditional" and "Style" Public Policy Challenges
Affecting the Democrats in the Race for the
Governorship in Ohio in 2006 Influenced by
Issues Related to the Election for President in
2008 26

CHAPTER 6   "The Art of Possible" Communitarianism
Linked with Liberal Democracy. 31

CHAPTER 7   Grassroots' Voter Contacts and Communicative
             Response Venues: A Revolution in
             Communication. 33

Part II   *Pragmatic Grassroots Reality-Testing*

CHAPTER 8   "The Train Has Left the Station" Outdated
             Thoughts from the Past: the RepublicanParty's
             Agenda for Ohio 39

CHAPTER 9   "Take Back Ohio" Progressive Ideas to Establish a
             Covenant with the People of Ohio and the Office
             of the Governor 40

CHAPTER 10   The Future Role of Labor Unions Influencing the
             Democratic Party and the American Voter. 41

CHAPTER 11   Four Key "Traditional" Issues influencing the 2006
             Governor's Race in Ohio as well as the Election for
             President in 2008. 42

CHAPTER 12   Seven Key "Style" Issues Influencing the 2006
             Governor's Race in Ohio:. 44

Part III   *Where we are as a Country, and why the*
             Campaign of 2006 for Governor in the State of Ohio
             is Crucial for Ohioans and the Nation...

CHAPTER 13   A Ten—Twenty Year Projection of Choices for the
             State of Ohio as Part of Our Global Village
             Commitment. 49

CHAPTER 14   Essential Political Grassroots Communications and
             Response Mechanisms: A Summary. 51

CHAPTER 15   A Final Checklist Testing a New Paradigm Shift
             Affecting Voter Decision-Making Choices. 53

CHAPTER 16   Projections: Circa, 2006, 2007, 2008, and
             Beyond. 58

CHAPTER 17 What the Democrats Forgot to do in 2004 and
Can Be Corrected in 2006 and 2008............60

CHAPTER 18 Three Battleground Strategies for the Democrats to
Win in Ohio in 2006: What Needs to Be Done 64

CHAPTER 19 County Politics in Ottawa County, Ohio:
A Microcosm and the Epicenter of the State 66

CHAPTER 20 A Case History of the Events Leading to the
Senator Max Cleland Town Meeting, December 1,
2005 70

CHAPTER 21 Ten Strategies for the Democrats for the
Twenty-six Battleground Counties of Ohio for the
2006 Governor's Race.......................73

CHAPTER 22 Six Definitive Paradigm Shifts in Democratic
Strategies for Voting Behavior Choices (Winning
with Sweat Equity) 76

CHAPTER 23 Preventing election Fraud at Local, State, and
National Levels of Government: The Ohio Example
2004–2008 78

APPENDIX A proposed National Symposium hosted at
Put-in-Bay, Erie County, Ohio.................79

Selected References 81

Selected Bibliography 85

Websites to Win Back the Governorship in Ohio in 2006 and the
White House in 2008..........................89

Glossary 91

About the Authors.............................93

Acknowledgements

I would like to thank the many, many people who have contributed to this guide, which became a succession of critical readers engaging in true "democracy." I would particularly like to acknowledge Mr. Michael Herron and Mr. Robert F. Davis. Their specific ideas and comments helped me to focus my view of politics and voting behavior as seen through different viewpoints.

Mike Herron helped me to focus on politics through the eyes of a different generation than mine. The perspectives he articulated enabled me to provide political issues which are significant to blocs of voters.

Bob Davis articulated concepts that renewed my faith in what legal immigration should mean in our multi-cultural society, and what could be potentially known as *The United States of the Americas—(a blending of a mixture of cultures, representing an 800 year old European influenced Mesa-American culture, of continued development on the continent of North America.)*

He further helped me to understand how the establishment of a moral status with universal rights and privileges, representing a true world class of citizenship standards revered by all the cultures of the world, is within the realm of viable possibilities.

I am greatly indebted to both of them.

For the sake of improved citizen involvement and participation, we must all work within this ever changing grand experiment known as the American democracy.

In this two year quest to research and write this book it has not been easy to live with me. It is further not easy to live with anyone who has the "disability" of Attention Deficit Disorder. I am not, however, referring to the Republican state legislators in Ohio or to the members of Congress, or to the President of the United States when it comes to the crisis in our government today as it relates to the oxymoron called "deficit financing" through Treasury bond borrowing or pension funds invested in speculative rare coins, i.e., the Thomas Noe Coin Deal scandal in Ohio!

I am, in fact, referring to my own situation, which is both a blessing and a challenge related to creativity, innovation, and social awareness. As seen through the lens of diminishing political egalitarianism facing the citizens of our country, and the demise of the shrinking middle class, with so much and so many options, this disability has been both a help and a hindrance!

I fervently believe that the purpose in writing this book is the belief that one person, one citizen, if he or she takes a proactive role and the responsibility of being a citizen of this great democracy of ours, can truly make a difference!

Vernon Lucas Albright,
September, 2006

Preface

This guide develops a series of grassroots strategies to win the governor's mansion for the Democratic Party in 2006. By recruiting a cadre of dedicated "Worker Bees"—interested civic minded Democrats, "independents" and concerned Republicans, this goal can be accomplished!

This Guidebook assists in achieving the goal of electing Congressman Ted Strickland as the next Governor of Ohio in 2006. It is this author's belief that the philosophical concept of egalitarianism, coupled with access to political leaders, required and enhanced political ethics and leadership traits including leaders' feedback responses through citizen involvement, **will** make a difference. The development of these types of political relationships can allow for the voters of Ohio to "Take Back Ohio" and return it to the people of this state with responsible and effective governance.

This preface outlines what this guide is all about, and how to use it. It is recommended that the following eleven steps be implemented to accomplish the goal of electing Congressman Ted Strickland to be Governor.

1. There are essentially twenty-six[*] key Democratic counties in the state of Ohio that are crucial to winning the governorship in 2006: Ashtabula, Athens, Belmont, Clark, Columbiana, Cuyahoga, Erie, Franklin, Hocking, Jefferson, Lake, Lorain, Lucas, Mahoning, Marion, Monroe, Montgomery, Ottawa, Perry, Portage, Sandusky, Seneca, Stark, Summit Trumbull, and Wood. Intense "Worker Bee" grassroots penetration must take place in all of these bellwether counties in order for the Democrats to win.

2. Screen and select an initial number of professional staff members, including a paid "Director of Volunteers" to provide ultimately consistent, standardized

---

[*]   Because of extra efforts on the part of selected "Worker Bees" in the counties of Ottawa, Marion, Perry, Sandusky, and possibly Seneca, a plurality in Democratic Party votes may be able to be obtained for the Congressman Strickland candidacy.

training for everyone involved in the campaign, and a paid "Coordinator of Volunteers," for each of the battleground counties.

3. Remember, initially, that although the goal is to win the governorship in 2006, its overall impact nationally will be profound indeed in determining who the next President of the United States will be in just two years.

4. Nominate five persons per battleground county to create individual citizen "Political Action Committees," i.e. Focus Group participants with membership represented by: (1) a party official or staff member designated by the elected official (2) those strongly identifiable with the Democratic Party (3) those "leaning" to Democratic Party values and support its issues (4) "Independents" reflecting a "grassroots" voting behavior personality that is "independent" of either party and (5) "Undecided"—those who need to be motivated by "worker bees."

For polling and research purposes, each group would be weighted by a factor of 4%, totaling 96%. The responses and efforts of these focus groups could result in gaining twenty electoral votes in 2008.

5. Choose a steering committee composed of "Key Political Educators" representing a synergistic Executive Board of Directors composed of Congressman Ted Strickland (Democratic Party nominee for Governor), Darrell Opfer (Democratic Party nominee for state representative for the 81st state house district of Ohio) and Ginny Park, Ottawa County Recorder, and two "Worker Bee Politicos" to coordinate the issues of these twenty-six battleground counties, and to assist the paid Director of Volunteers to manage and organize these teams of "Worker Bees."**

6. Learn how and when and where to set up the system of an additional group of five "Captains" for the purpose of increasing voter registration from among five prototype lists: (1) a Democratic Party County Board of Elections Official (2) an

---

**   It may initially require a series of grassroots political successes in order for the hierarchal leadership of the Democratic Party to agree to participate in some type of centralized party control and coordination. If this proves to be the case, the initial composition of such a synergistic Executive Board of Directors may at first consist only of a state-wide "paid" Director of Volunteers, a series of non-paid regional volunteers, and three ad-hoc worker bees selected for each of the twenty-six battleground counties that could indeed act as a stand-alone pragmatic political concept, to be in place by September 5, of 2006 (the day after Labor Day).

individual who is a "Strongly-Oriented Democrat" (3) an individual described as a "Leaning Democrat" (4) a individual labeled "Independent," and (5) an individual labeled "Undecided."

7. Establish teams of five, to determine the selection of other "worker bees." Based on 19th century style caucuses, but using the internet to recruit and implement, a network of "host" worker bees can be created from this base. This is grassroots democracy, using twenty-first century technology to its fullest! All of these teams of "worker bees" must be in place no later than September, 2006.

8. Gain feedback responses to improve, update, and rewrite major tenants of this guidebook on an ongoing, trial-and-error, bi-weekly basis.

9. Expand upon the implementation of using key electioneering strategies formulated by both the national DNC, the state Democratic Party, and ideas generated at the local county levels by the "worker bees." Individual meetings, group conference calls and in-person seminars, coupled with feedback responses via faxes, e-mail; special administrative political strategy meetings, and internet chat rooms to improve this Guidebook and the "Game Plan," with access to political strategists in order to formulate, improve, and correct significant flaws that will become apparent in a campaign of this nature; and **consistency** among all will increase the chances of winning the Governorship in 2006—the only goal for these meetings, through specific interaction and implementation processes. Only time, success, and the degree of acceptability will determine the outcome for such a challenging as well as innovative grassroots form of citizenship involvement as seen from the eyes of the entrenched party officials and their respective staff members.

10. Quantitative verification of results related to voter registration and turnout from the 2004 Presidential results in Ohio will be essential to this project. A list will be delivered by the state Democratic Party headquarters in Columbus to the campaign manager of the Eighty-first state representative district and to the Director of Volunteers for the purpose of registration, voter turn out, and additional volunteers needed as field workers during the final three months of the campaign: September, October, and November, using a district-wide series of canvassing and follow-up procedures.

11. Develop a list of one hundred "worker bees" for each of the twenty-six battleground Counties and allow for reasonable access to the key staff workers, includ-

ing party headquarters in Columbus. A Prototype contact list would include the following contact source data:

Key Grassroots Networking Contacts (N=100+)

Name: _____   _____ _____

Voice: _____   **Fax:** _____

Address: _____

E-Mail: _____

Web Site: _____

PART I
An Introduction to Winning Elections

1

Guidelines for Democrats to Win the Governorship in 2006

The following represent the suggested guidelines for the Democratic Party to follow in order to win the governorship for Ted Strickland in 2006:

(1) THE OHIO STRATEGY: 2004-2012:

A Crucial State Needed by Both Parties (20 Electoral Votes)

Registration and successful turnout could reverse the near tie (less than 60,000 votes) that occurred in Ohio during the 2004 Presidential election

Ohio is divided into eighty-eight counties, distinctly demarcated between the urban North and the rural South.

If Democratic registration is increased by only 2% and corresponding voter turnout of 2% is gained by the Democrats in November for the eight northern counties of: Lucas, Ottawa, Erie, Lorain, Cuyahoga, Stark, Summit, Mahoning plus Franklin County in the center of the state, and by a very small percentage in seventeen targeted "other" counties, then the scales could tip in favor of the Democrats in 2006.

Higher turnout from Democrats while managing other factors such as polling places, booths, lines and other such disputed conditions, will be critical in affecting the election in 2006. The capability of the Democratic Party to win in November will indeed represent a vote of self-confidence by the voters of Ohio with the accomplishments of these goals. However, before specific political strategies can be considered for the year 2008, the all important governors' races must first be won by the Democrats in 2006, thereby increasing their influence on the 2008 Presidential election just two years away.

(2) FOCUS GROUP STRATEGIES

The purpose of these focus groups and sample survey research strategies is to hold a series of five non-partisan political rallies and major stump speeches in which the Democratic candidate for Governor, Ted Strickland, will articulate pre-determined topics of local, state, national and international significance in randomly selected timeframes to a predefined audience composed of Democrats, Republicans, and Independents, based upon vote totals and representative sample sizes gathered from Presidential voting patterns in 2004.

The following format is representative of the twenty-six defined battleground counties in Ohio, and reflects the goals of this strategy. Time-value focus groups during September, October, and November, 2006 will be crucial, and efforts on behalf of the Strickland Campaign can make a significant difference.

One part of this strategy is to make inroads in the minds of grassroots voters and their friends concerning the quality of issues to be discussed, a qualitative and quantitative improvement over the old system. In future years, there will be better tools of analysis for all candidates concerned with the ultimate life of this concept and strategy.

This is not to suggest that the old political methods of primaries and a general election should be scrapped. Implementing this approach would act as a measuring tool only, to better guide each of the Party candidates in addressing their individual campaigns. Creating a better perspective and public policy programs, with insight hopefully gained by being a more effective politician representative of the overall concept of "American Democracy," and the concerns and wishes of grassroots registered voters of these twenty-six bellwether counties, must be addressed beforehand in order for Congressman Strickland to be the next Democratic governor.

In the weeks and months to follow, the implementation and development of such a strategy will be outlined in greater depth, will be field tested on a county-by-county approach, hopefully to help win the governorship for Ted Strickland in November, beginning this process by September 2006.

Major Components of this Strategy

Components of the major elements of such a series of strategies will be:

(1) major issues to be discussed during the 2006 campaign

(2) analysis of voter attitude and perception of each of the major candidates

(3) better understanding of the uniqueness of each of the twenty-six counties surveyed and their overall influence on the election for governor

(4) new "worker bee" strategies formulated at the grassroots level of politics in Ohio to reflect the preferences of the people surveyed, based on county-by-county conglomerate swings in the voter decision-making process as well as outside state influences from large anonymous political consulting groups centered inside the "D.C. Beltway"

(5) review of potential "outside" world events influencing these bellwether counties, as well as the rest of the state

Each week a report will be generated of the operational inputs and outputs of these ever-evolving strategies. These battle position reports should represent two types. One will be that of "for your eyes only," confidential reports made available only to the candidates themselves in order not to disclose highly sensitive information which the other party might be able to use as a counter strategy, and two, general but insightful information to be considered for release to the media as opposed to attack ad types of news releases! Overall communication between the coordinators of the field work bee staff would be recommended highly without either side feeling discounted as to the overall goal of "keeping your eyes on the prize."

NORMATIVE RULES FOR WINNING THE GOVERNORSHIP IN OHIO IN 2006

Three Major Normative Rules of Political Conduct:

Rule #1: *There is no guarantee that any single county can ensure a victory for the Democrats in 2006.*

Rule #2: *Expect the unexpected and always plan for the unexpected.*

Rule #3: *Scenarios for the eight battleground counties of northern Ohio, Franklin County in the center of the state, and the "other" seventeen key battleground counties could well represent the best chance for the Democrats to win the Governorship in 2006.*

In any political campaign, alliance groups are ever-evolving, and always changing. Strategies must be anticipated and redesigned to provide for contingency plans, to keep the opposing party on the defensive. Policies such as moral "style" issue positions and initiatives must not only excite the average voter, but also unite them into blocs of political support for demonstrable projects such as technologically sophisticated training programs, the establishment of local health care clinics, and expanded bicycle paths for commuting and pleasure, thereby helping to increase voter registration, participation, and turnout.

The successful campaign will "think outside the box" of the status quo, and anticipate new circumstances and conditions as well as strategies to confront scenarios which may never happen. The skill is to develop and react effectively to impeccable networks of communication which produce invaluable information about the grassroots' citizenry belief patterns and systems involvement at the local levels in Ohio is crucial. It is no longer a choice of simply making more campaign promises and not delivering when elected.

The savvy political strategist must develop plans to engage and involve voters; to allow them to participate in grassroots projects such as the ones mentioned above, designed to mobilize vital support. They must be quickly adaptable to changing and unforeseeable circumstances, and key players. These projects could engender identification with the Democratic Party, and a possible return to the fold. Updated and ever-changing "Voter Profiles" must be firmly established once again, no later than September 2006, and be constantly adjusted to fit each specialized circumstance.

Examples of Survey Research Methodology as Part of Ongoing in-the-Field Research Projects

The following examples of survey research techniques will suffice for this aspect of the analysis, and allow the reader to implement needed assessments that each of respondents must have, in order to be certified as a codified sub-sample electorate. This valuable component will have a composite rate of thirty percent added to that of the top "political gatekeepers" representing elected state and local officials from Ohio with a weighted average of seventy percent, totaling 100%.

It will be the combined weighted averages equaling 100% that will allow this investigator to analyze and initially guide other "worker bees" across the country helping to analyze future elections, which will assist in choosing a Presidential nominee. The beginning of a Presidential election process, as seen from the viewpoint of those of us who are sufficiently interested in grassroots politics, as well as a concerted dialogue between one's elected policy-making elite and the man on the street who really believes he has something to say about his responsibilities in becoming a future grassroots activist known as a "Worker Bee Citizen Activist."[*]

Participatory Forms of Observation

Necessary insights should now begin to be realized starting in September, 2006 on a trial-and-error basis, in order to perfect these techniques of electioneering and voting behavioral analysis. They will be elaborated in greater detail with the publication of future editions of this book, or in added appendices with later publications.

Various components which comprise the study for ongoing field research are essential. One must remember that ongoing field research is based upon local

---

[*] Please contact this writer by Email to obtain questions to be used for this work, as well as updated techniques used in the field of survey research methods with necessary input and analyses to make projects like this viable in becoming reality-tested for voter decision choices in "Winning the Governorship in 2006" and "Winning the White House in 2008 and Beyond." (lukeandmary@sbcglobal.net.)

political happenings in the twenty-six battleground counties, as well as outside events that must be constantly evaluated in order to make this series of political strategies work, and to become a reality for winning the governorship in Ohio in 2006.

The Republican Party will work just as hard to achieve their goal to retain the governorship for their standard bearer in 2006, and for the events leading up to this process.

This will be especially true regarding ideological as well as organizational political support teams, generated by members of the conservative religious churches and their followers in southern and rural Ohio.

2

Age, Demographics, and Policy Issues (Ages 18 to 100+)

The following observations concerning age, demographics, and policy issues represent this writer's hypothetical analysis of issues related to specific age groups.

Ages 18 to 25

Turnout of voters between the ages of **18 to 25** will be critical for Democrats. Their primary concerns revolve around the impact that the following issues have in their lives:

1. Potential re-establishment of a "backdoor draft," especially for members of the Ohio National Guard serving in Iraq

2. Paying off their student loans

3. Quality education for themselves and their children

4. Job opportunities and career direction

5. Ability to ensure quality life in support of their parents (one generation helping out their parents' generation)

Ages 25 to 35

The next age and demographic group will be voters between the ages of 25 and 35. This group I would call the "getting started and staying grounded" group. Their issues are:

1. Start-up costs for housing purchases—the American dream of home ownership

2. Continuing to pay off persistent student loan(s)

3. Concern with governmental plans to provide them with any type of future Social Security benefits or financial security for their retirement years

4. Finding a suitable life partner and starting a family

Ages 35 to 45

This age group is known as "the getting established and staying focused" group, with all types of family and interpersonal issues, such as maintaining job stability, home ownership, and affordable health care. The specific issues of this group are:

1. Finally paying off their student debt or finding a job that "pays good money" for the next twenty years in an ever-increasing and changing global economy

2. Buying their first home, or a better one for their next purchase

3. Learning a new skill, trade, or earning a graduate school degree to help secure their future in a global economy

4. Continuing to find a suitable partner through marriage or remarriage

Ages 45 to 65

The concerns of this group are:

1. Proper planning to ensure a "protected retirement" including health care

2. Educating their children

3. Continued concern about a "backdoor draft" affecting their children

4. General issues of race and religion

5. Specific issues related to religious beliefs and religious tolerance for the other guy's views, and

6. Family and fiscal responsibility as it relates to local and state issues, versus federal budgets and governmental spending patterns integrated with total financial monetary and fiscal planning

Ages 60 to 70-75

The concerns of this group are represented by:

1. Protecting Social Security benefits

2. Lowering the cost of prescription drugs

3. Long-term health care insurance

4. Mentoring and Volunteerism
   (Projects related to their grandchildren and the other children of the world)

5. Adequate leisure and recreational activities, coupled with environmental concerns such as global warming

6. Fiscal responsibility and conservation of the federal budget and how it relates to domestic spending versus international protection from terrorism

Ages 75 to 80-85*

This demographic age group of potential voters is known as the "middle years" in a growing cycle of senior citizens between the ages of 75-85.*

This group represents a very dynamic and very potentially healthy group who are concerned with these three major issues:

1. Cost of prescription drugs

2. Protecting Social Security Programs and what's left of their private pensions

---

* Senator John McCain, if elected President, would be in this age group while in office!

3. Long-Term Care Insurance protection as major economic/dignity factors

Ages 86 to 100+

The final age and demographic grouping are still active in our society; these are the potential voters ages 86 to 100+. This is the fastest growing demographic group in America today. This group is concerned with two major issues:

1. Continuation of Volunteering and Senor Mentoring Programs as "receivers" as well as "givers" of such services

2. The quality of healthy life remaining for them in their "golden years"

3

Watch your Backsides and Beware of the... "Moral Majority"

Key factors affecting political outcome are campaign issues divided into two major categories:

(I) "Global Policy" Issues

(II) "Moral Values" Questions

The strategy to successfully gain the political capital from the coattails of these, and other, issues is critical. The real art form and genius in political manipulation is in the ability to link certain policy issues with certain moral "style" issues, so that voters will vote in a particular way; conversely, to neutralize these kinds of issues to the extent that they may not be as important as basic bread-and-butter domestic and economic issues, or significant foreign policy issues. In the long-run, this will have a pronounced impact upon which voter decides to vote for which candidate.

(I) POLICY ISSUES

There are approximately six and a half billion people inhabiting our planet in 2006. Of these people, approximately one billion speak English with Spanish as a second language; conversely, one billion speak Spanish with English as a second language. One billion speak Chinese.

(1) In order to communicate effectively with at least one of every two people during the next twenty years *throughout* our global village, it will be necessary in the

future to speak all three of these languages, with English as our national language. (2) We live in a global village in the Twenty-first Century, not just a series of isolated and provincial communities that have continued to turn their back on the rest of the world.

<u>Policy Issues from a Global Perspective Affecting Ohio Citizens</u>:

Educating all of the children of our global village to minimum standards over the next twenty years has been discussed eloquently by Thomas L. Friedman in his book
The World Is Flat—A Brief History of the Twenty-First Century
(Farrar, Straus and Giroux, 2005.)

To quote Friedman:

"I cannot tell any other society or culture what to say to its own children, but I can tell you what I say to my own: The world is being flattened. I didn't start it and you can't stop it, except at a great cost to human development and your own future. But we can manage it, for better or worse. If it is to be for better, not for worse, then you and your generation must not live in fear of either the terrorists or of tomorrow, of either al-Qaeda or of Infosys. You can flourish in this flat world, but it does take the right imagination and the right motivation. While your lives have been powerfully shaped by 9/11, the world needs you to be forever the generation of 9/11—the generation of strategic optimists, the generation of more dreams than memories, the generation that wakes up each morning and not only imagines that things can be better but also acts on that imagination every day."

(II)
<u>Candidates Running for the Office of Governor in the State of Ohio Should Answer the Following "Moral Values" Questions:</u>

1. What is your position regarding "compromise" legislation built into "executive solutions" regarding the Supreme Court decision "Roe v. Wade"?

2. What qualities and moral values do you incorporate into future leadership roles assumed by a younger and more enlightened generation of political

leaders who will assume leadership in the state of Ohio locally, as well as nationally?

3. Do you believe this question is a moral value question that needs to be answered in the affirmative: "Living in the United States today means that (Circa: 2006) every American citizen working fulltime should receive a minimum "Living Wage" of $10.00 an hour?" And please provide what steps you would take to make this moral crusade a reality for all Americans during your first year in office, if you believe this to be the case.

The Illusions from the 2004 Presidential Election and How They Relate to the Campaign and Race for Governor in Ohio in 2006

"The Emperor has no clothes."

A sitting President during a war has never been defeated. A sitting President having a plurality in the rural counties and small towns of the United States is also difficult to defeat. And without the wholehearted support of the vast majority of the Hispanic vote nationally (60% or better, not 56% as was the case in 2004), coupled with significant defections from the black minorities from the urban areas—defeat is certain!

An unbeatable coalition of a rural turn-out-the-vote campaign empowered by a "minority" candidate with a 51% disapproval rating, and represented by a minority Republican Party registration list of potential voters, which was able to take away the election from the smugly biased Eastern-oriented leadership wing of the Democratic Party was due to the superior organizational skills of the Republican Party, and not of one's ideological viewpoint over that of the other political party's views.

The Democratic leadership did not properly train its group of transported highly dedicated amateur kids, who were matched against a group of seasoned professionals and volunteers over 65, recruited locally. These kids proved to be no match in a very closely contested election. It appeared that the Republicans wanted to win more than the Democrats did, at the grass-roots level, where it counted the most.

Outsourcing in many ways is not beneficial for a local or national economy, and certainly does not make much sense when it comes to the recruitment of quality talent from the local grassroots level. The "Boys and Girls" soldiers for Senator Kerry did not stand a chance in their goal to get out more voters on Election Day, compared to what the Republicans were able to do.

What is needed now, and not achieved in 2004, are more paid professionals and older volunteers, especially those between the ages of fifty-five and seventy, to campaign for the Democrats. The Democratic Party has asked too much from its hardy band of idealistic college students, and strong labor union help, to do it all. As with the Children's Crusades of the eleventh century, for which Pope Urban asked for a "Child's Crusade," these 'children' were slaughtered at the Gates of Jerusalem (the polling booths in the state of Ohio)!

The Definitive Media Images of the 2004 Presidential Election and the Lessons to Be Learned for the Race for Governor in Ohio in 2006

One should contrast the character traits of any future candidate for President or Governor to that of any of the candidates for Governor in 2006, and those candidates who wish to run for President in 2008.

On one hand, the American people were given the stereotypical Senator John Kerry from the liberal state of Massachusetts, represented as an East Coast Liberal Snob, who believed in idealistic causes which had been perceived by the American people as not being truly tested.

Also, related to the "equal rights doctrine for all," which was perceived by some to be at the expense of the majority, and worked against the "Protestant Ethics and Values" of hard work thought by many of the working poor to be their espoused value system, this became a wedge issue which resulted in votes for President Bush in 2004. (Lakoff, 1980, 2003)

The Presidential candidate George Bush, although receiving a negative fifty-one percent disapproval rating from the American public, was cast by some "political insiders" as a "spoiled rich kid" that played his "Hispanic card" of being the former Governor of Texas, who spoke Spanish but was not Hispanic, and came from a non-working environment in which all of the money that he ever needed was given to him by his political party "fat cats," any tine he wanted it, and then some.

The President was also accused of coming from a type of environment in which he never worked a day in his life, never held a "real job," flew jet planes in the State of Alabama for the Alabama National Guard and not in Vietnam, partied a lot, drank a lot in his early years, found religion but was, **nevertheless,** *a Sitting Wartime President.*

The perception of the American voter in 2004 was that President Bush believed in the fundamental values of the American family more than his opponent, Senator Kerry. He believed in the almighty power of God more than his opponent, was a "Born Again Christian," which Senator Kerry was not, and kept the American people "safe from terrorism attacks in the United States" accordingly to the popular image needed to win the Presidency—real or unreal, as projected by the spin masters that surround this President.

President Bush convinced the American voter that his policies prevented the terrorists from attacking America on American soil after 9/11, was not a "flip/flopper," and was strong and resolute to bring the terrorists to justice. He was also married to a sweet and lovely wife named Laura, and was "the lesser of the two evils." This was the message presented, and he won, and Kerry did not!

With these two popular stereotypes in mind, and with the barrage of ceaseless political charges leveled by the Republicans and unanswered by the Democrats, keeping the Democratic Party constantly on the defensive, the candidate and the rank and file of the Party were truly overwhelmed by the Republican's war of words and the Democrats' ineffective "war of word" in reply. They could not connect with the people who mattered, the disenfranchised voters and the "independents." The Republican attack ads did, however, energize the "Religious Right" with stylized messages to bring out their numbers from the rural counties and to tip the balance in the key battleground states of Ohio, Iowa, New Mexico, Nevada, Colorado, and Missouri.

Any win, in the case of Ohio, or in the two states of Iowa and Missouri, or in the three-state combination of New Mexico, Nevada, and Colorado, would have resulted with a Kerry win in the Electoral College. It was indeed, a very close election and it was <u>not</u> as the Republicans are fond of saying a "landslide mandate" for the President. It should also be noted on November 3, 2004, 135,000 provisional ballot votes were still left to be counted in the state of Ohio. These uncounted votes would not win the election for John Kerry, but these votes when counted, would have probably made the results even closer in that state.

And this would have meant that possibly the results were decided by less that one-half of one percent by the voters in Ohio! This was not a "landslide," and this was not a significant "mandate." It was, in reality, a brilliant piece of "marketing" that persuaded 50.7% versus 48.3%, and the other part of America who decided to "wait 'til next year" or 2008, and voted the remaining 1% third party. Some of the other voters who had still expressed a disapproval rating for the President in various opinion polls before the election, voted for him anyway, or so it seems.

This gave President Bush a thin plurality in the count of 18 electoral votes needed to reach the "magic" 270 total to win the Presidency in 2004. (http://en.wikipedia.org/wikiU.S._presidential_election, _2004)

In the long run, there are no formal degree programs in either Education, Political Science, or Public Policy to obtain the pragmatic experience to become a great decision-maker, with the skills necessary for the job of Governor of the state of Ohio or for that matter, President of the United States.[*]

It becomes, however, a very long process for an exceptional person to undertake this great political adventure. Ted Strickland, in this writer's opinion has passed the entrance exam to be qualified. The only matter remaining is a final approval from the voters of Ohio for him to be the next Governor of Ohio.

The ability to follow and learn and actually thrive from such on-the-job-experiences in politically elected and appointed offices, indeed, can significantly benefit the individual with the challenge and the opportunities to serve his country and the world. Strickland will now be able to accept this responsibility in January, 2007.

---

[*]   In his book, *The Capacity to Govern* (pp.124-125) Professor Yehezkel Dror does propose that such a related series of programs be offered to higher level senior officials in government, and public policy-making officials!

Bipartisan Political Centralism

These old attitudes of "perceived negative extreme liberalism" must be changed by providing a positive effort and effect through centrist leadership policies based upon our multi-cultural society. We can all do better, and this is how we are going to do it, is based upon the principles of "reframing," (Lakoff, 2004), the images espousing sound moral family values, reflecting the hopes of a reconstituted Democrat Party, inclusive of its centrist political philosophies, and not the radical extremes of either the right or the left. Protecting the rights of all minorities as well as serving as a beacon of hope and purpose by developing bi-partisan compromises between the Republicans and the Democrats is what will win this election in 2006 as well as 2008.

4

A Series of Value Systems for Case Studies in Ohio Representing Changing Family Value Systems Over the Next Generation ("Style" Challenges—Family and Community Moral Issues Affecting the Democrats and Republican Value Systems)

Fourteen key *"style"* (moral) issues affecting the 2006 general election for governor of Ohio should complement the academic training and experience that Congressman Ted Strickland possesses, having been educated in family counseling and obtaining a doctor's degree from the University of Kentucky in this field.

This is how the Democrats stand in stark contrast to the "Republican theory" of government:

1. Freedom of Partnership Choice (Democrats) versus negativity concerning Gay Rights (Republicans)

2. Pro Civil Union Partnerships (Democrats) versus Anti Same-Sex Marriage (Republicans)

3. Pro-Choice (Democrats) versus Anti-Abortion (Republicans)

4. Comprehensive beliefs in a Christian philosophy to aid the poor (Democrats) versus Totality of Fundamentalist Christian Belief Systems—pulling yourself up by your bootstraps, without bootstraps (Republicans)

5. Belief in Divine Inspiration in the Creation of the Universe (Democrats) versus "Creationists" Interpretation of the Bible (Republicans)

6. "Charity to all and malice towards none" (Democrats and 'Lincolnest' Philosophy) versus "Good versus Evil" from a Fundamentalist viewpoint (Republicans)

7. Belief in God as a Spiritual Concept (Democrats) versus Belief in "God" as a theistic concept only (Republicans)

8. The secular evolution of human society (Democrats) versus "The Second Coming of Christ" (Republicans)

9. Monogamy (Democrat and Republican Western Christian Value System) versus Polygamy (Islamic religious teachings)

10. Belief in "Forgiveness and Understanding" (Democrats) vs. Belief in "Hell and Damnation" (Fundamentalist Republican)

11. Separation of Church and State in the Public Sector (Democrats) versus Advocates of Public School Prayers (Republicans)

12. Belief that Human rights on a global scale will replace international terrorism as the key globally oriented issues (Bipartisan)

13. "The internet [as a technical and socialization tool] will further isolate the poor, and/or the internet will help create greater regional democracies—raising the question of whether [these] two trends are ultimately reconcilable." (Wallis, 2005, p. 370). (Non-Partisan)

14. The politics of Communitarianism versus the secular politics of liberalism (Non-Partisan)

An entirely different slant is presented in Jim Wallis's book, *God's Politics* (*Why the Right Gets it Wrong and the Left Doesn't Get It*). It is this writer's belief that Mr. Wallis's twenty-seven options represent an exhaustive but nevertheless comprehensive list of issues on which the Democrats really need to focus in order to truly become the "party of the people" and have a true globally-based social consciousness:

1. Faith in the new millennium will be defined much more by action than by doctrine.

2. Concurrently, religious fundamentalism will continue to rise in the face of moral decline.

3. Women in leadership in every area of life will become commonplace.

4. Overcoming poverty will become the great moral issue as we move [further] into the new millennium.

5. The number of spiritual progressives will grow.

6. The challenge of pluralism will replace the challenge of secularism as many diverse religious and spiritual traditions have to learn how to live with one another.

7. More parents will choose good books over mindless and soulless television.

8. The enormous and growing gap between the rich and the rest of us will finally be recognized as a real problem for both democracy and religion, shaking up our two party politics (which is really only one party of the rich and the powerful).

9. The movement that started with the Jubilee 2000 campaign will ultimately succeed in eliminating the Third World Debts, which realistically can never be repaid.

10. Fair trade will become as important to us as free trade.

11. Nuclear weapons will become a big issue again, but the real question is whether anything will be done about them, until a city is incinerated [or a city is biologically destroyed].

12. Human rights will replace national sovereignty as the key international issue.

13. Wealthy countries will become inundated with immigration unless the North/South economic divide is faced.

14. Something like the Marshall Plan, which rebuilt vanquished nations after World War II, will be created for the developing world.

15. More and more affluent families will get off the pressure train and adopt simpler lifestyles.

16. More churches will throw their arms around at-risk kids, but it won't be enough until society/societies put children first.

17. Faith based organizations will become critical partners in forging new social policy, but will tell government that they can't solve poverty by themselves.

18. The need for prophetic religion will grow.

19. Television will get worse and more people will decide they don't want their reality to be like reality TV.

20. Radio [and the internet] will become more and more important as an alternative media.

21. In the Catholic Church, there will be married and female priests, and the importance of lay and female leadership will continue to grow.

22. Peacemaking and conflict resolution will be regarded as among our most highly valued skills.

23. We will have to learn much more about forgiveness and reconciliation if we are to heal violence.

24. Wal-Mart will sell us everything unless citizens as consumers act strategically to restore a genuinely free and diverse marketplace and support a revitalized labor movement.

25. The Left will decide, as the conservatives already have, that the ideas are important and will begin to offer some better ones.

26. Hope will be the most essential ingredient for social change.

27. Raising children will be seen as the most important occupation. (Wallis, 2005, pp. 368-371)

In summary, if the twenty-seven moral issues can be combined with the more traditional public policy issues, Ted Strickland will have a much better chance of capturing the Governorship in 2006.

Local and State Issues

The following, in outline form, represents as a brief snapshot for future discussion related to counter-strategy used by both sides in the contest for Governor in 2006:

Type "A" Policy Issues:

1. "Living Wages" reflected by quality jobs in one's local and state communities, buttressed by tax credits for those families of the working poor who fall below the poverty line (same as 'Type "B" Moral Issues)

2. The local environment and natural disaster relief

3. Local education initiatives and referendums

Type "B" Moral Issues

1. "The Moral Concept of the Living Wage"
    (Policy and Moral Value Issues)

2. Abortion to protect the life of the mother

3. Gay Rights and freedom of choice

4. Gun Control and the specific choices under the "Right to Bear Arms"

5. Civil Union Partnerships

The Unfinished Democratic Advocacy Plans for the working men and women of the *United States of the Americas* is an ongoing agenda continuing from 2006 through 2008, winning the governorship in 2006 and continuing to the eve of the election for President in 2008.

This political sea will change over the next two years and beyond, but will retain these variables:

1. Hope versus Fear

2. "Living Wages" versus personal depression and economic despair for the underclass, the working poor, and the shrinking middle class

3. Volunteerism versus ethnocentrism and "do nothingness"

4. Strategic and Cooperative Alliances throughout the world versus a "Go it Alone Neo-conservatism policy"

Which will be the more powerful policy issues, and where will Local, State, Regional, National, or International issues be used as campaign tools, as they relate to the 2006 race for governor? These questions still represent a grave challenge for the Democratic Party of Ohio to "Take Back the Governorship" and return it to the people of Ohio.

Testing Four Hypotheses Needed to Win the Governorship

A hypothesis to test these four variables of this topic is: all four of these issues must be proactively addressed convincingly by concerned citizens in concert with "moral" politicians for each region or country—especially the twenty-six bellwether counties suggested above.

Each of the carefully selected twenty-six battleground counties in Ohio must be further studied, and citizen grassroots involvement must be implemented now! Also, it should be noted that the impact of these "moral" and ethical issues could become so significant that they override other strategies to recapture the White House as early as the end of 2007.

Time waits for no one!

5

"Traditional" and "Style" Public Policy Challenges Affecting the Democrats in the Race for the Governorship in Ohio in 2006 Influenced by Issues Related to the Election for President in 2008

The first fifteen public policy points listed represent political issues which must now be considered discernable dialogue points to make contact with the voters and political decision-makers in Ohio, as well as across the nation.

Key questions must be asked about what the "Local Politics" are, and how to listen to the answers, the needs, desires, and "wish lists" of the people from local areas, with regional perspectives becoming very important in building grassroots support and establishing cadres of influence.

These issues are discussed not only from a local level based upon voter perceptions, but also from a broadly based area of national significance. Fourteen key issues regarding domestic and foreign policy issues are also listed, which should also be critical in deciding the outcome of the 2008 Presidential election and future elections over the next twenty years.

A whole new generation can benefit from these guidelines of civic participation based upon an active civilian participatory society.

The following are issues which transcend the local and state issues, but nevertheless impact all Ohioans:

1. The preliminaries for a concrete policy for a "flexible" plan of staged-withdrawal from Iraq implemented concurrently by the United States government and the government of Iraq, by the end of 2006.

2. United States Energy Independence from <u>all</u> imported Middle East oil, as well as sources coming from Russia and Africa, where the peoples living there are continuing to be exploited by despotic regimes of indifference.

    There will also be built-in environment protection laws developed each year as required targeted goals over the next ten years. They would be coupled with the establishment of joint venture projects with Brazil and Cuba for the development of their renewable sugar cane crops as the fuel of choice to power transportation and industry throughout the Western Hemisphere.

3. Public Policy Recommendations affecting America's global public policy immigration programs to be determined by a state referendum in 2008.

4. Preparation and effective response mechanism protecting the lives and health needs for all American citizens facing personal and natural disaster.

5. Winning a series of unending battles against radical global terrorism with distinct global value and ethos systems, over a time frame of two generations, based upon global cultural considerations.

6. In-sourcing job opportunities and "Work Enhancement Skills" during the First Quarter of the 21st Century, versus outsourcing and downsizing, a result of wage imbalance coupled with poor domestic academic and training skills as well as a decline in the development of persons able to use entrepreneurial skills admitted through the reduction of immigration quotas for people coming to the United States, or through domestic programs designed to encourage the development of these skills.

7. Revamping Health Care Services in the United States as well as globally to represent universal healthcare based upon the specific choices of individuals, extended families, and institutional care settings for standard-

ized quality improvement and effective delivery systems as well as prescription drug programs based on need, not exclusively income.

8. The establishment of Non-Governmental and Not-for-Profit Foundations that create Multi-Cultural Language Study and Comparative Religion and Moral Philosophy Centers at grassroots levels for the purposes of understanding the positive philosophies of the great religions of the world as well as the dangerous and negative aspects of all religions, when compared historically to the present for the development of a truly modern foundation for ethics and spirituality.

    These institutions would be secular, civic minded, humanistic, and neutral ethos non-biases in nature, based upon some of the major guidelines recommended by the late Joseph Campbell[*] and recognize the need based upon global ethos value systems provided through early childhood, in cooperation with global student education and childhood learning facilities with student exchange programs.

9. Student and Senior Global Education Exchange Programs, with tax credits associated with these exchange programs.

10. Establishing pilot projects for the development of the Concept of "Global Senior Mentoring and Volunteerism" Programs and its impact on the American psyche.

11. A Series of Family-Based Moral and Self-Improvement Programs to be placed before the American people based upon a "Quadrennial Referendum Initiative" time frame, voted county-wide as well as statewide.

12. "Rural American Centers" in Ohio which influence global Initiatives, affecting the economy of the United States and the world economy, especially in the area of technology and innovation, based upon new innovation in manufacturing products from around the world.

13. Establishing a fair and equitable Tax code in Ohio and for America.

14. "Saving" Social Security, Medicare, and Medicaid with established safety nets linked with additional advisory alternative private savings accounts with built-in Security Exchange Commission monitoring systems.

---

[*]   Please google "Joseph Campbell" on the internet for greater details.

15. Global Warming awareness projects coupled with the establishment of a whole new generation of "green" environmentally safe business developed domestically at the local, state, national, and international levels with standards related to preventing environmental degradation.

Major Public Policy Needs Perceived by the American Voter

Like it or not, we Americans now live in a global village; and what happens somewhere else in our interdependent world now has a major impact upon our daily lives, directly or indirectly. In chapters to come the above issues will be reduced from twenty-four issues to six policy issues and two style issues. Eventually as in any political campaign, as it heats up, four, three, or fewer issues of the day emerge.

And the concentration in the public's mind revolves around these two, three, or four "bread and butter issues."

Mainstays of Projected Key Issues Relating to the 2008 Presidential Election

Some things in politics do seem to remain constant. And these issues tend to revolve around these four common themes:

1. Economic Job Security and Educational Opportunities for all of America's two-paycheck and single-parent family system

2. Personal health care, and a safe environment, within an environmentally sound planet

3. Adequate and affordable shelter for all sectors of our society thereby helping to put a stop to urban decay and the social destruction of our inner cities, the historical mainstays and support centers of the Democratic Party

4. War and Peace issues related to international terrorism fostered by living in a global village

Please remember that this is an ongoing, quarterly-updated handbook, subject to change, based on weekly and quarterly changes happening in our world.

Two Major Public Policy "Style" Issues

The two major "style" issues most likely to be discussed in the 2008 Presidential election could be (1) family values and (2) ethics associated with public office and office holders. Both of these issues will be difficult to focus upon as related to either political party, or how the American voter will make their final decision the day as he or she steps into the voting booth and makes the ultimate decision as to who will be the ethical and inspirational leader selected to guide the American people, and influence the rest of the world over the next four years.

The whole process starts now in Ohio as the fall election campaign for governor begins in earnest in September!

6

"The Art of Possible" Communitarianism Linked with Liberal Democracy

The following six concepts represent a foundation needed to become fully equipped as a grassroots campaign worker. These critical concepts can, in the long run, establish a better informed decision-making process favoring the political philosophies of the Democratic Party. These political philosophies will benefit the Democrats only if a truly nurturing process can begin to become a way to identify what Rosamund Stone Zander has outlined in her book "*The Art of Possibility*."[*]

Each of these six approaches are self-contained in instructing better grassroots campaign workers, and also serve as a definitive way to establish a team of workers linking together, united in order to get the job done in each of the twenty-six battleground counties being contested by both parties.

These are the six self-contained gyro-systems to establish the "The Art of the Possible":

1. The Value of Political networking through the concept *"it's all invented"* (*What assumptions am I making, that I'm not aware I'm making, that give me what I see?"* (Zander, 2000, p. 15)
    To be effective in this regard, the manner in which issues are framed is critical.

---

[*]   Rosamund Stone Zander, *The Art of Possibility*, New York: Penguin Books, 2002; pp. 15-139.

2. The fulltime political "volunteers," with a minimum three years of voter contact experience, (*"stepping into a universe of possibilities"* Zander, 2000, pp. 17-23)

3. Grassroots political communitarian participation seminars (*"Giving an A"* Zander, 2000, p. 42)

4. Tutorials on "Election Balloting" and procedures to protect against "Election Fraud" (*"Being a Contribution"* Zander, 2000, p. 99)

5. Volunteer "Manpower Temps" as a worker substitute for the voter in line on Election Day, so that the voter doesn't lose wages as well as child and family care providers during this time (however long it takes to vote!) (*"Lighting a Spark"* Zander, 2000, p. 139)

6. Global public forums on television and the internet to receive input and insights as the responsibility of the American voter being a community and a world citizen ("Lighting a Spark" Zander, 2000, p. 139).

Any one of the above contacts and communicative response venues and mechanisms may prove to the right method and strategy in order to win the maximum amount of voters' approval and plurality in any particular election. In the great game of politics, however, the real art form in the process lies with which combination is the most effective to use locally, and in which region of the country? This concept of an ongoing political process and working hypothesis still remains one of the biggest challenges facing the rank and file citizen political grassroots activist!

A greater focus as to how this political process is implemented and evolves will be discussed in greater detail as this book unfolds. Changes will be made and updated as each revised edition is published and distributed to grassroots "worker bees."

These updates will focus on a state-to-statewide basis throughout the sixteen battleground states selected by this writer continuing during 2007 through election eve of 2008. (Circa: September, 2006)

7

Grassroots' Voter Contacts and Communicative Response Venues: A Revolution in Communication

Communicative Response Venues

The heart as well the salvation of American Democracy may well lie with how the American voter communicates with their state and local representatives, congressman, senator, or even the President. The fact of the matter is that in most cases he or she is still not able or willing to do this.

Approximately fifty percent of the American population does not even bother to vote, which gives the power over to those who do, or those who are in the right positions to influence governmental decision-makers.

This then leads to the question: what if a modification of this trend were to occur by those individuals who do vote, and also participate in a much more vigorous manner, by becoming the "worker bees" of politics?

By this I mean the door-to-door canvassers, the phone bank volunteers in a campaign, the home made sign-makers to be placed in the yards of middle America, and the homes of the working poor who do vote. And finally, those individuals who attend the old-fashioned town meetings held across this country of ours. Would this make a difference?

I think so!

The difference would be that with significant numbers of registered voters actively participating in grassroots democracy across political party lines throughout America, beg-a-thon campaign boiler rooms could be eliminated for the most part, with "worker bee" participation being able to markedly decrease the need for campaign funding and financial contributions, except from the fat cats of both political parties.

Therefore, it is this writer's belief and hypothesis that "political sweat equity" would then replace the insidious nature of most campaign contributions now supposedly needed in most political campaigns in our country.

It remains to be seen what the exact numerical correlation would be between the increases in worker bee activation and reducing the need for runaway political campaign "begging" financing. Data based upon all of these suppositions, however, can indeed be field tested this year and in 2007 and 2008, as well as in future political campaigns. With this in mind, future models of this scope can be used by other political operatives with their grassroots volunteer "worker bees" in order to work these types of key strategies into the political mix of modern day campaigns.

The Pivotal Roles to be Envisioned by Latin-American Communities, African-American Communities, and Asian-American Communities

It is imperative for Democrats to utilize the incredible potential of these three blocs of voters. To reach the hearts and minds and tap the talents of these Americans will be "where the action is" for many elections now and in the future. The demographics show that with a combined population of 25% Hispanics, approximately 14% African-Americans, and 11% Asian, this bloc of people of color will now represent the majority of Americans who are citizens of the United States within the next twenty to fifty years. (Hochschild, 2005, p.70)

Specifically, three of the four upcoming key gubernatorial elections involve major population groups of Hispanic-Americans, (author's note: Ohio at present lags behind this national demographic change, but not for long) and it has been determined that the outcome of these three "other elections" in 2006 will greatly influence the election of 2008. The Hispanic population makes up 22% of the citizens living in Colorado, 26% in Nevada, and 42 % in New Mexico. The other key race is Ohio which has an African-American population of 11% and a 1.5% Latin-American/Hispanic population.[*]

To summarize, the battleground states of Ohio, Colorado, Nevada and New Mexico are, in this author's opinion, the most important Governors' races in the nation to be held in 2006. The Democrats have a good chance to win at least three of these elections, and stand a very good chance to win the White House in 2008. (Circa: September, 2006)

---

[*]   As an anecdotal observation, however, is that this writer attended a high school graduation in 2006 in Leipsic, in Putnam County, and half of the class was Hispanic!

PART II
Pragmatic Grassroots Reality-Testing

8

"The Train Has Left the Station" Outdated Thoughts from the Past: the Republican Party's Agenda for Ohio

The following thoughts outline this author's opinions as to the general policy beliefs in Ohio, as represented by the Republican Party:

1. "Rugged individualism and 'pulling oneself up by one's bootstraps' is still the best way to succeed in Ohio's globally dominated economy today."

2. "The 'trickle down theory' of economics still works for a wage or salary earner in Ohio."

3. "Health care needs cannot be provided by the small business owner because it will put him out of business."

4. "Selling off the assets of the Ohio Turnpike is a great way to increase the revenue stream for the coffers of state government."

5. "A high speed 'rapid transit line' *out of the city* is a great way to encourage commerce in large metropolitan areas of Ohio."

9

"Take Back Ohio"
Progressive Ideas to Establish a
Covenant with the People of Ohio
and the Office of the Governor

1. "Believe me. If you learn anything about living in a chicken shack, it's that things can get better."

2. "The first thing we learn as small children is 'be nice to each other.' In other words, *care* about the other person. What a different world it would be if **all of us** could learn that lesson!"

3. "What we need is leadership willing to set our goals well above the horizon and the hard work and faith that it takes to get us there."

4. "Our great state is in desperate need of change, and I believe that I have the judgment, the vision, and the drive to lead Ohio to a new day."

5. "There is no state in the nation like Ohio! But like many Ohioans, I see a state that has lost its way. The Republicans have failed to lead us, putting at risk the future of our state's safety and strength."[*]

---

[*] These are direct quotes from the candidate, Ted Strickland, the Democratic Party's choice to be Governor in 2006.

10

The Future Role of Labor Unions Influencing the Democratic Party and the American Voter

Without massive support of the labor unions in 2006, the Democrats will not win the election! One of the major roles that a new, united, and revitalized labor movement can play during the 2006 gubernatorial election is the organization and participation of newly found members within this movement, to represent the working middle class that has lost its way in being able to compete in obtaining first class, high-paying, globally-based competitive jobs in a world-oriented economy.*

---

*   Reference: Matt Bai, *The New Boss*, N.Y.T. Magazine, 1-30-2005

11

Four Key "Traditional" Issues influencing the 2006 Governor's Race in Ohio as well as the Election for President in 2008

"Ted's [Top] Picks"

1. Affordable health care for all of the citizens of Ohio

2. Entrepenuarial training programs related to critical skill training

3. Energy independence from Middle Eastern Oil by the year 2014, through upgrading agriculturally-based production grown in our state and the development of bio-mass gasoline refinery plants in rural, agricultural areas, coupled with refining and bio-mass centers. These centers could be located in various agricultural areas of Ohio combining a strong agricultural base with that of a highly skilled working class population as in the example of Ottawa County.

"The Citizens' of Ohio Top picks"

1. Health Care

2. Available and affordable skill based training and internship programs for all students who are citizens of Ohio.

3. Available forms of fuels designed to compete in Ohio with the high costs of gasoline.

4. Tougher state laws to prevent pollution and global warming in Ohio.

"The Opposition Party's (Republicans') Top Picks"

1. Favor the rich by even larger tax cuts to this group, with increases in state programs in Ohio that promote "corporate welfare" tax-cutting schemes.

2. Opposition to increasing the minimum wage in Ohio.

3. Reducing restrictions on older environmental laws, in order to favor greater profits to large corporations.

4. Staying the course in Iraq [that involves us in a never ending sectarian civil war]

12

Seven Key "Style" Issues Influencing the 2006 Governor's Race in Ohio:

And the Winner is [according to this writer's views]…"The People of Ohio!" advocating the following:

1. Bring back the Ohio National Guard from Iraq based on a flexible withdrawal plan developed before the end of 2006, and allow the sectarian civil war to be settled by the Iraqi's themselves.   70% (estimated)

2. Affordable Education and training for Ohioans   70% (estimated)

3. Affordable Health Care for all Ohioans   60% (estimated)

4. Responsible Government   60% (estimated)

5. Tougher state laws to prevent environmental pollution and global warming   60% (estimated)

6. Active expansion of Ohio's outdoor hunting, fishing, bicycling, and recreational facilities.   50% (estimated)

7. Language competency programs encouraged by the state of Ohio representing the three major languages spoken in the world today: English, Spanish, and Chinese.*   (estimated issue interest unknown)

---

*   The development of early childhood education programs for children between the ages of two to six in private and pubic school programs would be developed in Ohio. This would encourage language skill proficiencies in two to three of the major languages spoken in the world today : English, Spanish, and Chinese. English would be confirmed in the State of Ohio as the national language.

This early preparation would allow the children of Ohio to communicate and compete on a more effective basis with the rest of the world as written and spoken communication patterns continue to evolve during the Twenty-First Century on a global basis. (A hypothetical 10% projected favorable response for this issue is estimated by this author throughout the state of Ohio.)

PART III

Where we are as a Country, and why the Campaign of 2006 for Governor in the State of Ohio is Crucial for Ohioans and the Nation...

13

A Ten—Twenty Year Projection of Choices for the State of Ohio as Part of Our Global Village Commitment

*A "Wish List" [suggested as this writer's opinion] for most Democrats, many "Independents,"
"Undecided Voters" and some Republicans:

1. The return of professional, skilled, technical, and manufacturing jobs to Ohio.

2. A body of elected officials that answers to the needs of Ohioans in the form of responsible, effective, caring, governmental services ("Citizen Based Audits").

3. Adequate and Affordable Health Care provided to all citizens living in Ohio.

4. Affordable education and training for all Ohio citizens, based upon competing in a global economy.

5. The development and implementation of a series of state proficiency examinations in two to three of the most spoken languages in the world over the next twenty years: English, Spanish, and Chinese in order to graduate from high school by the year 2016.

6. State of Ohio scholarships, internships, and exchange programs will be awarded to the top ten percent of High School graduates for advance study, training, and internships relating to future job opportunities with companies based in Ohio. Such a program would be funded with taxes imposed upon

Ohio-headquartered companies that have branches located around the world without paying taxes to Ohio.

7. Expanded state recreational facilities for hunting, fishing, bicycling, and other outdoor activities, all year round that emphasizes the quality of life encompassing Ohio's four seasonal changes, ambiance and climate (without hurricanes, earthquakes, or major forest fires).

8. These programs will start as immediate funded programs or as pilot projects beginning in the fall of 2007.

14

Essential Political Grassroots Communications and Response Mechanisms: A Summary

Voter Contacts and Communicative Response Venues

The following twelve political venues and contacts are discernable means to make contact with voters at the local and county levels, and in turn with the key political decision-makers who live within these regions. The question is, are all twelve of these commutative response mechanisms being used to their fullest capacity when working in concert with the "worker bees" in the field?

The following communicative venues represent specific areas needed for focused attention in order to understand that the "medium is the message." They are ranked by this writer in order of efficacy.

1. Door-to-door (village-wide, town-wide, and city-wide) canvassing based on follow-up, follow-up, and more follow-ups with centralized state based calls from Columbus phone banks with accessible cell phones doing "other" important "non-worker bee" things

2. "Starbucks" and rural "Coffee Shop" discussion groups, political "Meet the Candidate" events, "Worker Bee" house parties, College Seminars, "Worker Bee" book signing "Special Events" and news conferences, bipartisan Town Hall Meetings and County political caucuses

3. Dialogues at "saloons/local watering holes" and informal restaurants in urban and rural locations that support Democratic candidates, staffed by trained volunteers

4. The Internet, using authorized messages

5. E-mails, using authorized messages

6. Union Hall meetings and strategy sessions

7. Political radio talk shows/Religious radio programs, with close supervision

8. Television, with authorized messages

9. Newspapers, with authorized messages

10. Stump speeches and rallies (bipartisan events) coupled with flyers, direct mail, "county-based" phone banks and cell phones, all with authorized messages

15

A Final Checklist Testing a New Paradigm Shift Affecting Voter Decision-Making Choices

These three filtered policy issues represent the final phase of the 2006 gubernatorial election, as they may be determined by voter preference, public opinion polls, and small group focus sessions.

Traditional Public Policy Issues

The filtered three key "**Traditional**" (Policy) issues during the last three months of the 2006 governor's race in Ohio could be:

1. Pragmatic, new, global U.S. Immigration Policies and Procedures, and new guidelines for including the revamping of the federal government's response to domestic natural disasters

2. U.S. Student Global Education Achievement Goals

3. Fiscally Conservative Federal Budgetary Guidelines endorsed, implemented, and enforced by the American people.

Value and Moral Issues as they relate to political perception in the final stages of an election

The values and morals of Masculinity and Femininity as they relate to Hispanic American, African American, and Asian American, Ethos identification at the dawn of the multi-cultural value systems representing the beginnings of American Globalization Awareness has now begun.

A New Philosophical Political Value System and Globally-Oriented Paradigm Shift Related to People of Color

In many instances, the philosophy of Western values is associated with "equal rights" for males and females; equal opportunities existing for both, neither is discriminated against, and each has the right to treasure the opportunities to be "male" and to be "female," each is respected and appreciated.

The early 19th Century settlement of the "Midwest" was not populated by teenage girls or boys being sent by their parents to a soccer camp for the summer, somewhere in beautiful rustic Ohio! The settlement of the Midwest in nineteenth century America meant risk-taking by strong males and strong females, coupled with nurturing family values!

This is especially true for the taming of the Great Black Swamp that covered all of Northwestern Ohio in the nineteenth century! This has now been extended figuratively into the Twenty-First Century, to mean investigating challenging economic opportunities for Ohioans, to develop a balanced export-driven economy, on a global basis.

There will not be equal opportunities for all, at first, when competing in a global economy; but respect for what a man and woman from an equal as well as a gendered based value system, can indeed become apparent. Could such a system, however, still protect the rights of both men and women, while at the same time not sacrificing the values of the American Middle Class? ("Reframing the Issue" Lakoff, 1994)

I believe this to be true!

Remember that the founding fathers of our nation were fifty-five fully educated male social innovators and risk-takers, and their results, although not perfect, came about not by denigrating what it is to be defined as being a moral and ethical man. The moral strengths that made our country great remain represented in the strength of today's American family. What this means is respect for the women of America, who are equal partners in many ways, and who represent those striving for the goal of equal economic parity for all women throughout the world.

These goals should not, however, be gained at the expense of giving up the biological "hard wired" concepts of masculinity; and not at the expense of neglecting the evolution of progress, respect, trust, and cooperation between the sexes that has grown during the last forty years.

Masculine and feminine trust, demeanor and nurturing provided by fatherhood, motherhood, brotherhood, and sisterhood are all values and traditions which represent the American way of life and have been increasingly valued over the last ten to twenty years in our society.

The values associated with the progress that has been made in our country since the sixties for the protection of civil rights must not be taken for granted. These values and this type of progress are not accessible in many parts of the world today.

The State of Ohio Can Be a Model for a New Social and Moral Movement

Can the State of Ohio be used as a role model for the rest of our country? The people of Ohio are not engaged in a "war of the sexes" but they are engaged in a path of progress which could result in creating a true understanding of the social and family environment necessary to nurture and mentor the youth of America. Could both males and females be more responsible to the times and conditions of growing up with the concept of how to be a nurturing soul living in a "Globally Interdependent Village"?

The goal that young people be social as well as caring individuals, with separate agendas resulting from the dynamic differences between the sexes, needs to be better appreciated by us all. These concepts may indeed reflect the true meaning of men and the women with "Midwest" value systems in the guise of a new creative individual, birthed in those practical areas of life, representing a value system which is part of the independent-minded nature of our citizens living in the middle parts of America.

A new type of citizen is growing up during the first half of the 21st century, not only in the state of Ohio but in the rest of America as well. That individual is learning to accept and thrive in a global economy, subject to constant changes and innovations thrust upon us each day, whether we like it or not.

A citizen taking the best of the value systems from different cultures and saying at the same time: "I truly respect my friend in his independence and creativity, and will also agree with certain forms of progress and values representing a specific regional value system, that indicates how the West has granted freedom of movement, respect and opportunities for all."

The ethos of Ohio's Middle West values must include men accepting the responsibility of acting as key mentors to "lost boys from broken homes," and treasure and enhance the two-parent family as well as the single-parent families, for the strengths that they bring. A grave task continues to lurk, however, in our country.

How will we raise the thousands upon thousands of neglected children who are becoming more and more at risk, in an increasingly competitive global environment of work and responsibility?

There is indeed still time to accept the challenge of living in the global arena of educational achievements, entrepreneurship, and sportsman-like competition, coupled with the overall caring and bonding representing an emotionally strong male influence that continues to spring forth from the rich heritage that is still part of our culture of nurturing family values.

The challenge of mentoring youth in fatherless and/or motherless families throughout Ohio, and all of our country, has become one of the moral and cultural responsibilities for all adults to assume as our country faces new inward challenges to define leadership roles yet to be played on the world stage, during the first quarter of this century.

Through living in a global village, a culture which demonstrates a strong value system associating learning with how to become a mature man or woman, and also takes on the responsibility of becoming a citizen of our state, our country, and this planet can become the hallmark and agenda that our nation could be destined to accept.

President Franklin Roosevelt said during the darkest time of the deepest economic cycle of the world's greatest Depression in the 1930's the following:

"This generation of Americans has a rendezvous with destiny!"

Finally, learning how to become a giver of wisdom and to become a pillar of strength by being part of the brotherhood of mankind, as well as the brotherhood and sisterhood of humankind living in this value-laden multi-cultural world of ours is a task which must be accepted by all citizens of Ohio, and all of the other specific geographical regions of America with their variety of different value systems competing to be heard throughout the rest of our country, and in fact, *all* of the Americas.

16

Projections: Circa, 2006, 2007, 2008, and Beyond

Our society has now reached a crossroads as we begin a two-year countdown from now (2006) to the presidential election in 2008.

The issues that our nation and global society will be confronting within these next two years and in the ensuing sixteen years, may well determine the fate of all of humankind by the year 2028—the start of the next twenty-year generation of new leaders and new faces entering the political and social arenas of key leadership positions has already begun!

Through technology, the possibility of being able to interact effectively with anyone in the world today on a personal basis continues to be one of the major challenges faced by a modern society. Bridging the gap between having "big ideas" to ultimately realizing the implementation of these ideas into reality becomes a most daunting obstacle.

How can one network effectively in order to see that important ideas can be suggested for consideration at the grassroots level? How can these ideas be tested by translating them into a form of grassroots action-oriented public policy implementation forum for the betterment of our global village?

The need to emphasize local grassroots cooperation and regional harmony becomes the main challenge during the next two years, and that may be all the time that we have left to make a difference! Since all politics is local, no caring citizen should forget this admonition:

"For whom does the bell toll? It tolls for thee!"

The major goal of this "Pragmatist's Grassroots Playbook" has been to alert the reader to useful methods to win political campaigns, as well the hearts and minds of the American voter. Hopefully, a new dawn of freedom of choice may be upon our society, and a "Government of the People, we the people, by the People, and for the People shall not perish from this earth." [Lincoln's Gettysburg Address]

Finally, I close with a quote from Benjamin Franklin:

[We have a] "Republic, if you can keep it."

17

What the Democrats Forgot to do in 2004 and Can Be Corrected in 2006 and 2008

"Keep Your Eyes on the Prize"

Missed opportunities resulting in "My kingdom for a horse!" represent a series of epitaphs that the Democrats need to understand in order to win the White House in 2008.

Robert Reich wrote in his book *Reason* (Vintage Books, 2005.) that it's not merely attending another D.N.C. conference entitled "The Future of the Democratic Party" that will elect the next Governor, but rather that it is working [hard] at the grassroots level of politics that will really *count* this time around. This is what the Democrats did not do in 2004:

1. The necessary *turnout* among *registered* Democrats was not reflected in the results. Reliable data regarding actual turnout, particularly at polling places where machines were left in storage, people who left lines and reasons in addition to long wait, etc., is needed to determine what can be changed.

2. The Republicans simply *registered* and got more *new* voters *into the booth* than did the Democrats. Democrats did not convince those who were undecided, nor those who may have defected based on specific issue(s). Not only were Republicans more successful in convincing *individuals* in one-on-one exchanges, they made certain their votes counted through turnout.

3. The Republicans did a better job of managing the media; the Democrats did not produce "accurate, *'objective'* coverage (with favorable spin) media which could have garnered last-minute support.

4. The Republicans used "You're either with us or against us" extremely effectively. This approach alienated Democrats but *energized* the conservatives to support the Commander in Chief. Timely, focused, cohesive, consistent, response and retaliation to specific issues such as the Swift boat campaign, same sex marriage, gay rights, and abortion, fueled the faithful to passionately "defend the American way of life." The impact of the "moral majority" on the 2008 election is another case in point which will be discussed later in a future book yet to be written.

5. The election of 2004 was essentially a repeat of 2000, meaning the electoral vote breakdown and the outcome having been decided by one state. If the Democrats have a well-oiled machine *before* 2008, these results could be different. At present, this well-oiled political machine is missing the cadre of worker bees laboring passionately in the political vineyards of twenty-six key counties in Ohio that are critical in determining who the next governor of the state will be.

Voting Behavior Strategies to Consider

To win Ohio, it is critical that the Democrats capture 85% of the significantly heterogeneous Hispanic vote. This bloc permeates *all* of the battleground states.

Democrats need to bring forth effective messages and solid support *now* for issues such as social security, our enormous national debt and the impact of the balance of payment problems on budgetary outlays from outgoing revenue streams, represented by expanded entitlement programs of our aging baby boom population. These factors *will* be essential for this year's governor's race in Ohio, as the average voter votes from their pocketbook.

The 2006 election will reflect decisions based upon issues that relate to a domestic as well as global perspective. The Iraq situation will be completely different in November 2006 than it was in November 2004 or 2005. Technology brings the confrontation of the *world* to the p.c. and into the living rooms for all Americans. We first learned this in Viet Nam, and we have learned it over and over again since the war in Iraq began in 2002. (Circa: September, 2006)

It is time for Democrats to *educate* the average voter about the *impact* of the global economy which is now a reality, and about the technology that exposes us to other value systems that follow the opportunities of our worldwide economy. As migration patterns change, information and ethos value systems follow those who migrate to new areas of the world to better themselves, as well as the underclass poor beginning to migrate to other parts of the world and to Ohio, representing very significant numbers.

The reality of the 21st century is that America is not the *only* country with opportunities for an excellent education. America is not the only country in the world with "genius" level graduates, nor is it any longer the only country with unlimited economic opportunity.

As more and more people become more and more mobile in today's world, they take with them new and different value systems and standards of behavior. The challenge of this century is knowledge and a depth of understanding of the cultures, ethos systems, values, and standards of behavior of these migration patterns.

With ever-increasing travel and migration, these standards are increasingly diffused throughout societies, and for many reasons become more and more of the norm, rather than the exception. Cultural awareness related to the exchange of ideas and belief systems is incredibly heightened by many different people from many different regions throughout the world. The challenge we face is which values will be adopted and accepted; which one will dominate over the next ten years?

The current goal of American foreign policy to "provide the opportunity for democracy" in Afghanistan and Iraq is a case in point and remains to be seen. This trend of mobility and people-to-people exposure will only increase. The question of whether the spheres of influence of the fringe elements of fanatics who believe that their cause is *always* right will always dominate the greater numbers of their neutral/apathetic brethren is unclear.

Add to those without strong opinions, those without strong economic and/or political power, meaning the poor and the working poor, and the bloc in question becomes more and more significant, representing a time bomb of political upheaval just about ready to explode!

Major Challenges Facing the Democratic Party

Finally, it must be emphasized that speculation for a "blueprint for 'worker bee' involvement" such as this one to work, at a certain point in time is inevitably reduced to "being in the right place at the right time with the right political strategies," and the right skill base, and an incredible amount of luck. "Luck" has been defined as opportunity meeting preparation, but does there seem to be a confluence of circumstances and synchronicity which produces a winner?

Selecting the right candidate for the conditions at a specific point in that time of our history to favorably influence voters is the monumental challenge facing the Democratic Party today.

Generations yet unborn will be influenced by the decisions of the decade of our history following 2006. The rest of the world watches with fascination and wonderment (among other perspectives!) to see if our great experiment in civil society will endure. Will our government continue to function effectively for all of *us* both domestically and globally?

If anything is really remembered at all, what will history write about the governor's race in Ohio in 2006?

Progress belongs to nations able to adapt to change beneficial to all—not to a society longing for the good old days of small town rural America that lacks a world-view perspective representative of a modern "global village"!

This body of citizens known as Ohioans and a civilization known as the "United States of the ***Americas***" and its critical electoral decision-making process, added to the concept dubbed as "Penetrating Polarization," is still in the birth and development stage. Time is still available for this election process to give Ohio back to its people.

18

Three Battleground Strategies for the Democrats to Win in Ohio in 2006: What Needs to Be Done

The first set of strategies represents three projects this writer calls:

"Best Strategies Coupled with Political Realism for Winning the Governor's Mansion in 2006." These strategies revolve around the following issues:

1. What is a 'Political Landslide'? Answer: > than a 5% plurality for a victory

2. A Cautionary Tale about the lessons to be learned from the 2000 and 2004 Florida experience and how these lessons relate to the 2006 election for Governor in Ohio.

3. "It's the Economy [and the Battleground state of Ohio, based upon their core value systems] Stupid!"

In most political elections from an historical perspective, economic issues have represented the body of politics. The political trump card of economic issues, however, coupled with active and dynamic "worker bee" involvement over that of "religious political issues" could make the difference if economic conditions are right. Even so, the various strategies recommended in this book must be followed and coordinated with lock step precision with that of the hierarchy of the state Ohio Democratic Party.

If the Democrats are to win in 2006 and "throw the rascals out," the effective framing of issues that shows that the Republicans attempted to tamper with the Social Security safety net nationally, exacerbated the balance of payment problems, and increased in the federal deficit by spendthrift borrowing, thus resulting in enormous debts for our children and grandchildren, is critical. These three factors continue to be economic and political challenges facing our country nationally, and can also be demonstrated at the state level with what the Republicans have attempted to do with the Noe rare coin laundering scandal, proposals recommended on state capital gains tax cuts, and selling off the Ohio turnpike in order to gain a quick economic and political fix.

19

County Politics in Ottawa County, Ohio: A Microcosm and the Epicenter of the State

An Economic, Demographic, and Political Overview of Ottawa County, Ohio

Ottawa County, Ohio truly represents a unique chance to demonstrate what can be done at the grassroots level to win in the governorship for the Democrats in 2006. This county is located 19 miles East of Toledo and it represents the bedroom community next to Lucas County, Ohio as some residents commute to work each day.

This county is also comprised of small towns, farms, and one small city which represent part of the standard statistical metropolitan area of the greater Toledo-Lucas County, Ohio Area. Having a population of approximately 41,000 people, the next five years could represent potential growth of this county from a base of 41,000 people to 50,000. *

Such expansion would make Ottawa County a statistical representation of a truly metropolitan urbanized county in it own right!

---

* An ideal demographic breakdown would be to recruit three thousand residents to move to Ottawa County from the surrounding six county areas over the next ten years. An ethnic composition similar to that of the United States and is now under-represented, compared with the rest of the country would be this "ideal." It would need to be more sympathetic to the views of the Democratic Party and the wishes of the "Party of the People and the Common Man."

A class-oriented demographic composition would be as follows: Anglo-White Working Class skilled workers, Mexican-Hispanic Americans—the fastest growing population segment in America today, and African-Americans—the third largest population bloc (significantly underrepresented throughout the whole of Ottawa County.)

The new population figures at the time of the 2010 census could reach a figure of 50,000 if development were to proceed with increased tourism and recreational enhancements, expansion of service sector employment in the health care and retirement residential community sectors of bargain priced land, readily available for development in this county.

Further development of 21st century "Silicon Valley" types of industry capturing agricultural based bio-mass commodities available in Ottawa County, would be able to be processed locally in newly constructed fuel efficient refineries and would again allow the citizens of Northwestern Ohio to be competitive on the world stage in areas as well as similar counties in Ohio, to capture this type of economic comparative advantage. A competitive edge in commerce and trade on a global scale with the further expansion of industrial parks throughout the county and the growth and development of the port facilities of the City of Port Clinton, located on Lake Erie would once again be possible as it was in the Nineteenth Century in this region of the country.

This could truly mean the beginnings for the comprehensive development of this county and similar counties in Ohio. In turn, the potential of this county to become a modern comprehensive showcase for cosmopolitan urbanization could be achieved within the next decade!

A Further Geographical and Economic Profile of Ottawa County, Ohio

The Portage River runs through the center of Ottawa County. Port Clinton is the only city located in this county. The five largest employers in this county are the Davis-Bessie Nuclear Power Plant, The Brush Engineering Materials Company, Silgan Plastics, Lakewinds Industrial Park (county owned), and the Erie Industrial Park. These five major employers provide the potential to allow for quality growth and development in this area. The attainment of 1,500 new jobs, plus an equal number of employment opportunities in the surrounding counties, defined as part of this urbanized region of Ohio can make a significant difference in economic opportunities for all of the citizens living in this area.

Additional employment opportunities would also be found in newer computer design and enhanced areas of manufacturing, the expansion of the tourist industry on the southern shore of Lake Erie, and the expansion of related service industries linked to the health care field and the expansion of the numerous hospitals and health care retirement centers already located in this six county region of Ottawa, Lucas, Erie, Sandusky, Lorain, and Wood County.

The Political Landscape of Ottawa County, Ohio (circa, 2006)

Sixty-six yeas ago, Paul F. Lazarsfeld and his colleagues produced the first of many landmark studies concerning American voting behavior during the 1940 election. Ironically, Ottawa County adjoins Erie County, the site of the Lazarsfeld studies.

It is a site which all candidates running for the office of President need to study and analyze in order to better understand that this time it is for "all of the marbles" which includes "Winning the Governorship in 2006 in Ohio and the White House in 2008."

Key points to remember about winning Ottawa County:

In 2004, Erie County awarded John Kerry a plurality of 5.3%. In the neighboring county, Ottawa, Kerry lost by a plurality of a comparable 4.2%. Based upon a turnout of 23,000 votes projected in 2008 and the actual numbers that voted in the 2004 election, a mere 550 votes could elect Ted Strickland as the next Democratic governor in the state of Ohio. It is for this reason the challenge must now be met with hard work, passion, political involvement, and dedication on the part of new and seasoned political campaign volunteers over the next two months in Ohio and the next two years in critical battleground states.

A "political facelift" must be accomplished as soon as possible through communications, coordination, endorsement, cooperation, and funding from the Democratic organizations of Northwestern Ohio and the other battleground counties that represent the insurance policy for victory in 2006 for the Democrats.

A resident of Ottawa County, Ohio must be recruited as a professional (paid) Coordinator of Volunteers, reporting to the statewide Director of Volunteers. This Coordinator would begin working with the leaders of the Democratic Party immediately.

Printed materials developed for standardized training and performance expectations for everyone involved in campaigning efforts for the Governor's race is critical.

The preliminary structure of the campaign would include a minimum of five core "precinct leaders," recruited by the Coordinator, who would lead at least 25 to 100 passionate and dedicated volunteers to victory in 2006 and in 2008. Campaign training sessions should begin by after Labor Day, September 4, 2006 as a starting deadline!

Organization for the first annual Elmore, Ohio Labor Day 2007 Parade and Picnic with recruitment and correlated festivities that would influence not only Ottawa county, (the tail wagging the dog) but all of Northwestern Ohio. Such preparation needs to begin in September, 2006.

20

A Case History of the Events Leading to the Senator Max Cleland Town Meeting, December 1, 2005

After ninety days of trial and error preparation on this writer's part, Senator Max Cleland of Georgia consented to come to Elmore, Ohio to deliver a major foreign policy speech on citizenship, our international involvement in Iraq, and the economy of Ohio.

The results achieved were that ten percent of the entire population of Elmore attended (one hundred and fifty citizens). Definitive public policies were discussed, activation in the field of U.S. foreign policy in Iraq and the Middle East, coupled with a strong emphasis on grassroots citizen participation through the concept of a town meeting, and non-partisanship televised P.B. S. coverage were included.[*]

What made this event so challenging was that this writer was asking a well known political figure to come to a small town in Northwestern Ohio to deliver a major address, working with a fresh team of locally recruited "worker bees."

---

[*]   There were 150 individuals in attendance from a community of 1,500; ten percent of the total population in the immediate area. Toledo *Blade*, December 2, 2005. pp. 1& 2 (reported "100") *News Herald*, December 2, 2005, p.1 (reported "200") Contact this writer for online grassroots tutorials designed to duplicate participatory grassroots events in action: (lukeandmary@sbcglobal.net)

With today's busy American families who are overworked, overstressed, and over-scheduled, the first of many obstacles involved ways to motivate volunteer partic-ipation, in order for any potential political event to succeed is necessary.

The litany of things that had to be done involving the Senator Max Cleland Town Meeting is extensive. I should note that with the concept of the "worker bees" developed as it is now, the attitude and graciousness of Midwestern hospi-tality most definitely allows for this type of citizen involvement still to be accom-plished in this region of our country!

Thus, the following "political shopping list" represents truly a snapshot of crucial grassroots, and somewhat bipartisan, politics practiced in the Midwest:

1. The time-consuming details to arrange accommodations and personal ground transportation for a person who is extremely handicapped to come to a semi-rural area of Ohio, and to access and secure quite limited facilities adequate for his stay and this event

2. Having no money to stage such an event, ask total strangers and friends of the strangers not only to contribute to such an event, but to become part of the necessary recruitment process, come to the event itself, and help with their contacts to further organize the event

3. Arrange for all of the different types of media publicity for this event

4. Attempt to get several rival grassroots Democratic political factions to cooperate in order to co-sponsor such an event

5. Set a minimum goal of at least fifty "worker bees" to create and stage such an event

6. Secure the hall, school gym or school cafeteria location for the event at no cost

7. Arrange for PBS coverage

8. Secure sufficient commitment that the major newspapers would give adequate coverage to the event

9. Secure the cooperation and support of the local politicians to spread the word for support of the event and for them to attend as well

10. Obtain the crucial financial and personal support of the labor unions in the area

11. Live among the 'natives' with my wife and secure their trust and help for this and future events

12. Arrange for working dinners to host leading up to the event

13. Prepare a budget and work within the budgetary limits for such an event

14. Provide content analysis for an overall theme to make the event memorable

15. Put out any political fires or misunderstanding and alleviate any roadblocks and manage any setbacks leading up to the event

16. Continue to be enthusiastic, to remain goal oriented with an "eye on the prize" for the overall planning of the event

17. Arrange for online computer registration for such and event, in addition to canvassing and "cold" calls for citizens to attend, plus phone bank registration as well

18. Be somewhat bipartisan and keep the local Republicans happy or neutral, if possible—assuring them that there will be "Q&A" to challenge them to a meaningful dialogue; this can still be done in the Midwest!

19. Gain the support of the local business community for the event; use it to publicize the event with posters and word of mouth

20. Rehearse the agenda in advance; obtain the supporting speakers, and necessary county sheriff security arrangements

21. Work within a timeframe of sixty to ninety days to accomplish all of the above—paraphrasing Goldilocks' advice: "It can never be too hot, or too cold, but just right!"

Winning over hearts to commit to this event wasn't at all easy (especially Senator Cleland!) In fact, one of the state Democrats offered, after a local politico said that it should be cancelled if there weren't going to be fifty people there, that "They've never done anything like this in Elmore before."

Well, I agree with a Stanford professor who said "If you have a big idea, *do* a big idea!" Finally, for those who are interested, copies of the video can be obtained from the PBS outlet at Bowling Green State University, Bowling Green Ohio (WBSU).

21

Ten Strategies for the Democrats for the Twenty-six Battleground Counties of Ohio for the 2006 Governor's Race

Specific Strategies favoring the twenty-six Democratic Battleground counties are as follows:

1. Recruitment of a paid, professional "Director of Volunteers and Mentors" responsible for coordination and training of political volunteers must be implemented.

2. Remembering Howard Dean's two famous words in his opening remarks as the newly-elected head of the D.N.C.: "TURN OUT" is still the political clincher in any political campaign.

3. Programs to increase voting and balloting literacy among registered Democrats must be implemented on a continual basis.

4. Polling places with functioning machines, reasonable waiting times, and volunteers to provide both daycare and substitute temp work to retain wages for those workers taking off to vote, will ensure higher favorable turnout.

5. Local issue identification and challenges must be penetrated.

6. Significant increases in turnout for events which sets precedents for the election, with "word of mouth" volunteer recruiting of ("worker bees") keyed to selected internet websites is also necessary.

7. Widespread grassroots canvassing tied to the final two months of this campaign is crucial—September and October, 2006.

8. Effective cooperation among all factions and group blocs within the party is vital for political survival. "United we stand; divided…"

9. Garnering approximately 85% of the Hispanic vote will be necessary to win; currently 70% appear to be loyal to the Democrats. Leaving a critical factor of an additional 15% for the Republicans is not acceptable.

10. Voter turnout and predate/postdate verification is critical.

With these strategies as a preliminary checklist, a definitive process can begin to allow for a concentrated work effort consistent with winning on Election Day, which is less than two months from now! Much work must be accomplished, if the goal these goals are to become a reality by November.

Six Republican Party Strategies to Counteract

1. Recruit volunteers in a bipartisan manner from their new lists of "worker bees" in 2006, counteracting their lists developed in 2000 and 2004.

2. Continue to emphasize our own moral wedge issues (political framing).

3. Make sure that the Republican candidate running for Governor espouses real "moral value issues," and continues to call Congressman Strickland a "Liberal" (political framing) while the Congressman Ted Strickland, is able to call himself a "True Progressive from the Midwest"

4. Counteract regressive philosophies of neo-conservatism with that of the true nature of bipartisanship progressiveness as practiced in Ohio.
    In addition, it may be necessary to call "Blackwell's Backers" "Economic Royalists." (F.D.R., circa the 1930's)

5. Foster bipartisanship by working with the current Administration in Washington to win support for a peace plan for Iraq and the Middle East—instead of engaging in a go-it-alone strong "defensive" and "offensive" military commitment in these areas. This is what Congresswoman Strickland has advocated while serving in Congress.

6. The Republicans will continue to recruit and campaign from their base of small towns mainly in the southern and western rural regions of the state, countered by the contrasting agendas of "Worker Bees" focusing in the twenty-six battleground counties.

22

Six Definitive Paradigm Shifts in Democratic Strategies for Voting Behavior Choices (Winning with Sweat Equity)

In some cases the Republicans need not worry about upcoming elections, but in other cases they do. The following represent six issues that should keep the likes of Carl Rove up at night shaking in his boots and related "bootstraps":

1. Demographics for registered voters still favor the Democratic Party, as well as the well-organized "blog" machines coming from all economic and social classes with the extensive use of the internet, and specialized websites.

2. Realistic, pragmatic moral issues can effectively appeal to the target market areas of the lower class and the working poor of our country if the "framing" is correct. (Lakoff, 2002, 2003)

3. Immediate response from the Democrats to issues raised by the opposition in the example of the unsuccessful 2004 campaign "swift boat" issue proved be one of the detriments of the Kerry campaign, and is critical to any future campaign and must be counteracted by "politically framed" responses. (Lakoff, 2002 and 2003)

4. Foreign policy, while still very important for the political party in power facing re-election, becomes secondary to overriding domestic issues such as jobs, energy costs and protecting the local environment associated with global warming, and affordable, effective health care. These are just three examples of major areas of concern for the Ohio voter in 2006.

5. A grassroots wake up call from local citizens will begin to change the role of government, private enterprise, and the various functions of dynamic volunteerism by cadres of senior older adults willing to "Take Back America" based upon the egalitarian principle of "shared democracy."

6. Approximately 15% of the Hispanic vote currently seems to be leaning toward the Republicans; this number must at least be doubled, in order to influence the election in favor of the Republicans in 2006. This bloc is particularly significant in some of the twenty-six battleground counties of Ohio, and continues to grow. Counter recruitment drives by "worker bees" from the Democratic Party will be necessary for those who are fluent in Spanish; i.e. "*hormiga trabajadora.*"

23

Preventing election Fraud at Local, State, and National Levels of Government: The Ohio Example 2004–2008

Guidelines to be developed by the National "League of Women Voters" (non-partisan)

1. Adequate numbers of functioning voting booths that function on election day.

2. A paper trail receipt for each ballot.

3. Volunteer working temps, or baby-sitters to be provided for those individuals standing in line for more that 30 minutes.

APPENDIX

A proposed National Symposium hosted at Put-in-Bay, Erie County, Ohio

A July 3rd and 4th Holiday political Symposium in 2007 is neither farfetched nor inconceivable. The format of such an event would be to bring back the American family into the realm of innovative citizens' participation as a family unit in the concept of old-fashioned 19th century style politics.

Such an event would be a Fourth of July Holiday picnic both days, with hot dogs, pink lemonade, and ice cream. An array of high school marching bands and choirs, and other types of musical venues would perform. This event would be topped off by meaningful politic rhetoric from both political parties, and would culminate with the mandatory fireworks display each evening.

It would be a two day extravaganza, with the spotlight upon state and national politics. What has been accomplished by the new state Democratic administration in their first six months, and how the Republican Party, as the loyal opposition, has also helped to "Take back America."

Both our two main political parties will have to agree to participate, but this would truly be a grassroots politically awesome event! Those nominees receiving at least a 10% recognizable series of endorsements of "political support" from the five-time series of study focus groups, as well as the corollary 100+ "Political Advisor Opinion-Makers" list, also polled in the same time series, would be asked to attend and participate in this event.

This event would not be a political debate, but rather a political symposium showcasing the best of the ideas that each of the two parties has to offer the American voter.

Organization and preparation for an event of this type would be extensive and substantial. It is now time to get started with this plan, as time is of the utmost, and the beneficial results generated by such an event are needed for the sake of our country, as well as the rest of the world.

Selected References

Books

Allen, Cathy, "Crisis Management in Campaigns," Ronald A. Faucheux (Editor) *Winning Elections,* New York: M. Evans and Company, 2003.

Berelson, Bernard R., Lazarsfeld, Paul F. and McPhee, William N., *Voting,*

Chicago: University of Chicago Press, 1954

Bobbitt, Philip, *The Shield of Achilles,* New York: Anchor Books, 2002

Brunner, Borgan, *Time Almanac 2005 (with Information Please)* Needham, Ma. Pearson Education, Inc. 2004

Campbell, Angus. Converse, Philip, Miller, Warren, and Stoke, Donald

The American Voter, New York: John Wiley Sons, 1964

Campbell, Joseph. *The Masks of Gods,* Minneapolis: High bridge Audio Books, 2006 On-line Shoppers List Catalog.

Donovan, Robert J. *Conflict and Crisis (The Presidency of Harry S. Truman, 1945-1948),* New York: W.W. Norton & Company, 1977.

Donovan, Robert J. *The Tumultuous Years.* (The Presidency of Harry S. Truman) 1949-1953, Columbia, Mo: University of Missouri Press, (paperback edition) 1996.

Downs, Anthony, *An Economic Theory of Democracy,* New York: Harper & Row Publishers, 1957

Dror, Yehezkel, *Public Policy Reexamined,* San Francisco, Ca: Chandler Publishing Company, 1968.

Dror, Yehezkel, *The Capacity to Govern,* London: Frank Cass Publishers, 2001.

Frank, Thomas. *What's the Matter with Kansas?* New York: Henry Holt and Company, 2004.

Friedman, Thomas. *The World is Flat—A Brief History of the Twenty-First Century,* New York: Farrar, Straus and Giroux, 2005.

Josephson, Mathew, *The Politicos: 1865-1896* [out of print]

Kelley, Sarano, *The Game*, San Diego: Jodere Group, Inc., 2001.

Kent, Frank, *The Great Game of Politics,* Buffalo, New York, *Smith, Keyes, and Marshall, Publishers,* 1959

Lakoff, George, *Moral Politics*, Chicago: University of Chicago Press, 2002

_____, *Metaphors We Live By*: Chicago: University of Chicago Press, 2003.

_____, *Don't Think of an Elephant.* White River Junction Vermont: Chelsea Green Publications, 2004.

Latko, David W. *Everybody Wants your Money*. New York: Harper-Collins 2006.

Merton, Robert K. and Barber, Elinor, *The Travels and Adventures of Serendipity*, Princeton: Princeton University Press, 2004.

Modesitt, Jr. L.E. *The Ethos Effect*, New York, New York: A Tom Dorsey Associates Book, 2003.

Putnam, Robert, *Bowling Alone*, New York: Simon & Schuster, 2000.

Putnam, Robert, and Feldstein, Donald, *Better Together: Restoring the American Community*, New York: Simon & Schuster, 2003.

Reich, Robert. *Reason*, New York: Vintage Books, 2005.

Stoken, Dick. *The Great Game of Politics*, New York: A Tom Dorsey Associates Book, 2004.

Teasdale, Wayne, *The Mystic Heart*, Novato, Ca. New World Library, 2001

Wallis, Jim, *God's Politics*, San Francisco: Harper San Francisco, 2005.

Zander, Rosamund Stone, and Zander, Benjamin, *The Art of Possibility*, New York: Penguin Books, 2002.

Zinn, Howard, *Declarations of Independence*, New York: Harper Perennial, 1990.

Newspapers and Journals

Bai, Matt, "The New Boss*"*, NYT (New York Times Magazine Section), January 30, 2005

_____, "The Framing Wars*"*NYT (New York Times Magazine Section), (6), July 17, 2005

"The American Pie and how it was Sliced." Chicago Tribune (Section 2), p. 1) November 14, 2004.

Brook, David "What's on the Media Agenda" *In These Times*, Chicago, Il. December 13, 2004.

Fallows, James "Countdown to a Meltdown" (The Atlantic On-line) < www.the atlantic.com> July/August, 2005, pp. 1-26

Hochschild, Jennifer, "Looking Ahead: Racial Trends in the U.S." *Daedalus*, Winter, 2005 Vol 134, No. 1, p.70.

Jackson, Jessie. "What Strategy Should the Democrats Pursue?" *In These Times*, Chicago, IL. December 13, 2004.

Unpublished Documents

Albright, Vernon Lucas, *Presidential Voting Behavior in the Eleventh Legislative District of Baltimore County, Maryland: 1960-1964*, (Master Thesis, University of Maryland, 1967)

_____*An Evaluative Technical and Vocational Education Long-Term Planning Model*, Doctoral Dissertation, (formally University of Sarasota), Argosy University, 1980)

Selected Bibliography

Albright, Vernon Lucas. *An Evaluative Program Planning Model* (Unpublished Doctoral Dissertation) Argosy University, (Formally University of Sarasota: Sarasota, Florida. 1980.

_____. Presidential Voting Behavior in the Eleventh District of Baltimore County, Maryland 1960-1964. (Unpublished Master's Thesis0 The University of Maryland: College Park, Maryland. 1967.

Almond, Gabriel, R. Scott Appleby, and Emmanuel Sivan. *Strong Religion: The Rise of Fundalmentalisms around the World,* University of Chicago Press, 2003.

Bobbitt, Philip, *The Shield of Achilles*, New York: Anchor Books, 2003.

Collins, Randall, *The Sociology of Philosophies: A Global Theory of Intellectual Change.* Cambridge, Ma. The Belknap Press of Harvard University Press, 1988.

Deutsch, Karl W. *The Nerves of Government.* New York: The Free Press. 1961.

Dror, Y. *The Capacity to Govern.* London: Fran Cass Publishing, 2002.

_____. *Public Policymaking Reexamined.* San Francisco: Chandler Publishing, 1968.

Easton, D. *A System Analysis of Political Life.* New York: John Wiley, 1965.

Ellis, Susan J. and Jayne Cravens. *The Virtual Volunteering Guidebook.* Palo Alto, Ca.: Impact Online, Inc. 2000.

Faucheux, Richard A. *Winning Elections,* New York: M. Evans and Company, Inc., 2003

Fincher, C. "Planning Models & Paradigms in Higher Education." Journal of Higher education. (1972, Vol. 43.) pp. 754-767.

Finkel, Steven E. "Can Democracy Be Taught?" Journal of Democracy. (Oct. 2003, Vol. 14, No. 4) pp. 37-151.

Habermas, Jurgen. *Between Facts and Norms*. Cambridge, Ma. The MIT Press, 1998.

Haveland, E. "Transfer & Use of Trained Technology, a Model for Matching Training Approaches with Training Settings". Alexandria, Virginia: (HUM-RRO) October, 1974.

Jouvenel, Bertrand De. *The Art of Conjecture*. New York: Basic Books, 1967.

Landis, David. *The Wealth and Poverty of Nations*, New York: W.W. Norton, 1999.

Lazarsfeld, Paul F., Bernard Berelson, ad Hazel Gaudet. *The People's Choice*. New York: Columbia University Press, 1968.

Lippitt, G. L. *Visualizing Change: Model Building & the Change Process*. Fairfax, Virginia: (National Training Laboratories) Learning Resources Corporation, 1973.

Mahoney, Daniel J. *"Beyond the 'Prison of the Corollaries:' Liberty and the Common Good in the thought of Bertrand De Jouvenel."* The Political Science Reviewer. (October, 2003. Vol. 32) 93-117.

Morra-Imas, Linda and Ray C. Rist *"International Program for Development Evaluation Training."* Washington, D.C.: The World Bank, 2003.

Putnam, Robert D. *Bowling Alone*. New York: Touchstone, 2001.

Rawls, John. *A theory of Justice*. Cambridge: Harvard University Press, 1999.

_____. *Political Liberalism*. Cambridge: Harvard University Press, 1996.

Suchman, E. A. *Evaluative Research*. New York: Russell Sage Foundation, 1977.

Zeidan, David. *The Resurgence of Religion*, Herndon, Virginia: Brill Academic Publishers, 2003.

Newspapers, Magazines, and Journals

Bai, Matt, "The New Boss", NYT (New York Times Magazine Section), January 30, 2005

*_____, "The Framing Wars" NYT (New York Times Magazine Section), (6), July 17, 2005

_____, "Mrs. Triangulation" NYT (New York Time Magazine Section (6) September 2, 2005 pp. 62-67.

"The American Pie and how it was Sliced." Chicago Tribune (Section 2), p. 1) November 14, 2004.

*Boak, Joshua. "Ex-senator War Vet backs Strickland in Visit" Toledo Blade, December 2, 2005, p.2.

Brook, David "What's on the Media Agenda" *In These Times*, Chicago, Il. December 13, 2004.

_____ "Changing Bedfellows" New York Times, June 16, 2006 p. A23.

*Fallows, James "Countdown to a Meltdown" (The Atlantic On-line)
< www.the atlantic.com> July/August, 2005, pp. 1-26.

*Freidman, Jeffery. "Ignorance in Politics and Science" *Critical Review*
Volume 17, Numbers 1-2, (Winter-Spring 2005).

Gertner, Jon "Is How Much You Pay a Worker a Moral Issue?"
New York Times Magazine, Section 6, January 15, 2006.

*Hochschild, Jennifer, "Looking Ahead: Racial Trends in the U.S." *Daedalus*, Winter, 2005 Vol. 134, No. 1, p.70.

Jackson Jr., Jessie, 'What Strategy Should the Democrats Pursue?"
In These Times, Chicago, IL. December 13, 2004.

*Maizel, Boris "Why we Talk if we Disagree" *Critical Review,* (Volumes 17, Nos. 1-2, 2006)

*Montoya, Yvonne. "We Should Learn Lessons of Vietnam,' Cleland Says"
News Herald, Port Clinton, Ohio, December 2, 2005.

Correspondence

Letters and E-Mails to Senator Max Cleland Office of the United States Import-Export Bank, Washington, D.C. (2005)

Unpublished Documents

*Albright, Vernon Lucas, *Presidential Voting Behavior in the Eleventh Legislative District of Baltimore County, Maryland: 1960-1964*, (Master Thesis, University of Maryland, 1967)

_____*An Evaluative Technical and Vocational Education Long-Term Planning Model*, Doctoral Dissertation, (formally University of Sarasota), Argosy University, 1980)

Websites to Win Back the Governorship in Ohio in 2006 and the White House in 2008

Ohio Voter Election Statistics

Election.sostate.oh.us/results/RaceDeatils.aspx?race=PP.com

The 1948 Presidential Election

teachpol.tenj.edu/amer_pol_hist/fi?0000019a.htm

"729" political lobby help sites

moveon-help@list.moveon.org

Apollo Website

Appolow.org

Democratic 529 site

Moveon.org

Google

google.com

www.democraticunderground.com/discuss/
duboard.phpz=view_all&address=172x1

Glossary

A Glossary of Political Terminology

Caucus: An assembly of senior advisors. A political and social gathering, in a group setting, engaging in dialogue to determine direction of public policies and social issues

Communitarianism: Because of the large number of voters in modern democracies, elections provide for a greatly diluted form of political participation. Representative, indirect politics—with voters meetings and discussing and choosing at local level[s]—achieve some of the involvement in a political community which otherwise would be lost. (Ann Phillips, *Engendering Democracy* (Cambridge, 1991)

Ethos: The disposition, character, or fundamental values peculiar to a specific people, culture, or movement. (The *American Heritage Dictionary* (Second College Edition, (1991) Boston: Houghton Mifflin, 1991.

Framing: A linguistic way of looking at social and political issues which attempts to understand the unconscious desires reflected in a person's behavior that influences his decision, in contrast to the "rational man" concept to the contrary

Serendipity: "a natural gift for making useful discoveries by accident" (Encarta World English Dictionary, 1999)

Grassroots: The local regional people-to-people approach to citizenship and political participation

Mentoring: A program designed to have senior citizens train, educate, and evaluate the progress and growth of students, as young as pre-teenage years

Global Senior Volunteers and Mentors:

A cadre of dedicated citizens acting as volunteers acting in the capacity to help expand newer horizons for the people of the world who are in need of global style health, education and developmental programs in order to "live long nod prosper."

Guide: A tract or polemic designed to lead a particular individual or group to achieve a specific goal.

Social Capital: An economic approach to people-to-people capital formation development to achieve certain forms of political, social, and economic goals for the betterment of the community

Solipsism: the theory that self-existence is the only certainty, absolute egotism—the extreme form of subject idealism

"Worker Bees": Committed and inspired grass roots politically orientated citizen volunteers and advocates translated to mean,

Hormiga trabajadora, "Worker Ants" [in Spanish] (closest synonym for "Worker Bees")

About the Authors

BIOGRAPHICAL STATEMENTS

VERNON LUCAS ALBRIGHT, Ed.D.

Dr. Albright has spent twenty years as a Registered Investment Adviser and lecturer in public policy to grassroots volunteer organizations and academic institutions. He has developed programs in Honors Scholarship Mentoring Skills and College Program Planning, newer developments related to current technology in the fields of investment consultation, the development and implementation of electronic engineering technician programs, and training designed for the field of urban technology and public policy. He has also lectured to diverse senior centers on the subjects of long-term health care needs, international terrorism and personal financial security, worldwide volunteerism, global politics at all levels, and public policy-making.

CURRICULUM VITAE

Registered Investment Adviser, Albright Financial Services: Managing assets for scientists, engineers, college teachers, small business owners, and retirees. Philadelphia, Pa. and Chicago, IL. 1985 to present.
Independent Insurance Broker; Philadelphia, Pa.
Director of Admissions, Ross Medical University; Country of Dominica
Doctoral Degree Program, Argosy University
(formerly University of Sarasota); Sarasota, Florida
Director, REITs Electronic School; Toledo, Ohio
Admission officer, REITs Electronic Schools; Detroit Michigan,
Director and Instructor of Urban Technology Studies,
Washtenaw Community College; Ann Arbor, Michigan
Urban Planner; City of Toledo
Instructor of Political Science, Bowling Green State University;
Bowling Green, Ohio

Instructor of Political Science, University of Toledo;
Toledo, Ohio

EDUCATION:

B.A., Government; American University; Washington, D.C. Graduate studies in Sociology and Economics; University of Toledo Toledo, Ohio M.A., Government and Politics; University of Maryland College Park, Md. Ph.D. student, Political Science; Wayne State University Detroit, Michigan The University of Michigan Inter-University Consortium for Political Research; Ann Arbor, Michigan Ed.D., Adult Education and Evaluative Research;Argosy University (formerly University of Sarasota) Sarasota, Florida

MARY HELEN ALBRIGHT, M.A.

Ms. Albright has been the Director of Volunteers for the Methodist Hospitals of Chicago, Il.; Director of Admissions for the Valley Ridge Nursing Center of Bloomingdale, Il.; and Director of Patient Relations for the Northwestern University Children's Memorial Hospital in Chicago. Her experience in healthcare administration has provided her with broad perspectives in successfully melding the needs of the individual within the framework of the institution. Also a freelance professional editor, she has served in this capacity for two years as Editor for Albright Financial Services, a profit-making sole proprietorship.

EDUCATION

M.A., Health and Human Services Administration; Rider University Lawrenceville, N.J.

B.A., International Affairs; The George Washington University
Washington, D.C.

978-0-595-41070-5
0-595-41070-7